IN GOOD FAITH

IN
GOOD
FAITH

A journey in search of an unknown India

SABA NAQVI

Photograph courtesy: Aashim Tyagi

RAINLIGHT
RUPA

Published in RAINLIGHT by
Rupa Publications India Pvt. Ltd 2012
7/16, Ansari Road, Daryaganj
New Delhi 110002

Sales centres:
Allahabad Bengaluru Chennai
Hyderabad Jaipur Kathmandu
Kolkata Mumbai

ISBN: 978-81-291209-4-6

10 9 8 7 6 5 4 3 2 1

The moral right of the author has been asserted.

Typeset in 12/15 Adobe Jenson Pro at SÜRYA, New Delhi

Printed and bound in India by
Replika Press Pvt. Ltd.

This one is for Sara,
for a world of ideas, ideals
and compassion.

CONTENTS

MY FAMILY AND OTHER JOURNEYS

Real life is often a mess. But religion is usually described in absolute terms, especially in India where we look at religious identities through a political prism. We like to clear up the mess and prefer an uncluttered definition of what constitutes a Hindu or a Muslim. This may not always be an accurate reflection of religious and cultural identity in a country where vibrant little traditions have always survived along with the Great Traditions.

This work examines the several syncretic traditions that survive in India, largely amongst the Muslim community, but also with the participation of non-Muslims, within the cultural tradition of what may be defined as Hindu civilisation. It explores India's composite culture and perhaps perpetuates one of the greatest clichés about India—that it is a land of contradictions, dualism and pure chaos. There are no absolute truths here.

This book is also about a personal journey—a search for an India that is tolerant and safe for all communities, an India that synthesizes identities instead of atomizing us all into a Hindu atom here, a Muslim particle there, a Christian molecule some distance away, a Sikh on the periphery…

I call it a personal journey because I am the product of a mixed background and have always been fascinated by the manner in which identities are preserved and formulated. In my case, it is also the story of how identities are imposed by others and perhaps even by the politics of the country. This journey that I describe is as much a search for synthesis in the public domain as in the personal. It began twenty years ago, and it's taken me two decades to make sense of many things, internalize and understand the issues of identity that I was grappling with.

I must begin with the story of my family. My father comes from a Shia Muslim background rooted in a village in the Rae Bareli district of Uttar Pradesh and my grandfather practiced law in the state capital of Lucknow. Our family has always had a distinct culture and language, where the ideas of a composite culture have both been advocated and lived. There is equal felicity with classical music and the finer and complex expressions of great Urdu poets as with irreverent street poetry in the local dialects. There is also a heightened political awareness, as members of the clan—extended across little towns in Uttar Pradesh—have been split between an old linkage to the Congress party and ideological commitments to the communist parties. My grandfather's elder brother was the first Congress MLA from Rae Bareli, while my grandmother's younger brother was a communist. My grandparents were first cousins, so varying ideologies—from the nationalist to the radical— were accommodated in one family.

But no one was ever part of the Muslim League, although Mohammad Ali Jinnah's party was propelled by the Muslim landlords of the (then) United Provinces. Still, there is a section of the family that ended up in Pakistan as three of my grandmother's sisters married men who got jobs there. I am told that, at that time, they never imagined that the borders would be permanent. Many Muslim families with roots in India saw the Partition as a temporary estrangement.

So how do divided families evolve or keep in touch? I can only give the anecdotal example of my family. The Pakistanis hanker to come to India and visit their roots and when the visa regime relaxes, they arrive in batches, more flashily dressed, more made-up than us. At a superficial level, they seem different to my relatives in Uttar Pradesh who, I like to imagine, belong to the impoverished, intellectual elite (many are certainly impoverished!). Yet, in civilizational terms, I have found nothing to seek in Pakistan. I have visited thrice, each time for journalistic assignments. I have always found a great story but returned more convinced that the nation, whose name means 'Land of the Pure', was founded on a poor concept and is doomed because of its geographical location and the religious identity that the State has been culpable of promoting. Unlike most Indian delegations that visit the cities and return overwhelmed by Pakistani hospitality, I have, on occasion, travelled into the interiors with politicians like Nawaz Sharif, and each time felt very conscious of my gender amongst the sea of men, in regions where women are mostly in purdah and not seen in the public domain. The relatives in the cities of Pakistan are, however, always warm and loving (the women being very chic) and a separate book can be written on the divided clans of the subcontinent.

My mother Aruna's Protestant Christian family is a study in contrast to the chaos of the large Shia clan. Originally from Nasirabad in Rajasthan's Ajmer district, my grandfather was an orphan named Natha Singh who was educated by Christian missionaries and given the name Fazal Masih Nathaniel. He became the principal of the local school, then went to university in Edinburgh and returned to serve in the Delhi Secretariat. When he died at the age of forty-six (my mother was a teenager), he was the Director General of the National Employment Exchange. While Fazal Masih was an orphan, my grandmother, Ivy Martin, was raised in the biggest house in Nasirabad, still known as Peeli Kothi. The orphan and the girl from the big house fell in love, got married, moved to Delhi and had five daughters, the third being my mother, Aruna. Although his name was changed by missionaries, my grandfather gave all his daughters very Indian names such as 'Aruna', 'Nirmala' and 'Jyoti Chandramukhi'. But he died young and my grandmother had to fend for five young daughters. She started teaching a few students in her home. This exercise eventually expanded and she set up several small schools across Delhi. She also built a three-storey house in Safdarjung Enclave in South Delhi, which became our second home during my childhood.

Over the years, my Naani also became a religious fundamentalist. Earlier, the family belonged to the Free Church on Parliament Street but my grandmother slowly graduated towards the Pentecostal Church that advocates the process of proselytizing and harvesting souls. I had a child's eye view into a world of missionaries who would use my grandmother's home as a base in Delhi before setting off into the interiors to save native souls. The family was dismayed as this hysterical faith entered her home but as a child I found the missionaries hugely entertaining. I must add that, after my grandmother's passing, the family has reverted to the more genteel version of Christianity—playing Bach and Beethoven on the piano along with carols, and decorating a Christmas tree elaborately with loads of presents for the kids.

There is a charm in being raised without any one religious identity. My childhood was pretty anarchic on the matter of religious practice. Eid for us was a pocket money bonanza, but Christmas was the favoured festival as there was always a brightly-lit tree, presents and someone would dress as Santa Claus. We also lit up our house with great enthusiasm and burst crackers on Diwali and I always played Holi with my little gang of neighbourhood kids. Was there any special awareness that Eid should have been the primary festival? No, not at all. We visited relatives on Eid or they visited us and we collected Eidi—small amounts of money given by adults to children. In those pre-liberalization days, being raised by a school teacher mother and news reporter father, we were always broke and the money collected on Eid was a small fortune. If we were lucky, we got new clothes. But often, if there were no relatives in town, then Eid would just be a school holiday. We lived in a rented house in South Extension, South Delhi, not an area with any Muslim presence, so there was no sense of belonging to a congregational religion.

We were never taught to say our prayers or given any religious instruction about being a Muslim. My father's attitude to religious practice was shaped by irreverent Urdu poetry, his mother Atia's fine sense of language and aesthetics and perhaps her brother, S. M. Mehdi (called Mamujaan by all of us) who was a playwright, member of the CPI and IPTA and an intellectual influence on the entire clan. On many weekends we would be bundled into a Standard Herald car that we would push down the road before it sputtered to a start, and be driven to Karol Bagh in West Delhi where Mamujaan and family lived and, years later, I realized that some of the regular visitors there were celebrated poets and writers such as Kaifi Azmi and Majrooh Sultanpuri, among others. When I landed up in Bombay (now Mumbai) fresh out of college, broke, and on the lookout for a job, I remember writer Rahi Masoom Raza very kindly giving me a wonderful meal in his family home and offering to put me up because I was Mehdi's grand-niece.

I possibly absorbed the milieu in the family as I do cherish it now, but in the chaotic, democratic, large but unstructured clan that is my father's family, attention to detail was often missed. So it was entirely forgotten until it was too late that the children of Saeed Naqvi, who recited Urdu couplets at every pretext, were never taught Urdu. Every now and then, my father did publicly lament the illiterate state of his offspring and spoke vaguely about hiring a maulvi to put us through the letters of Urdu. But nothing was ever done other than the lapse in our Urdu education being occasionally noted. I don't think it ever crossed anyone's mind to teach us the Quran in Arabic.

Still, life was an education in the Naqvi clan. In Delhi we attended a good public school, but every summer holiday we were packed off in a train to my grandparents' home in Lucknow. Often my parents came for a brief while but then disappeared on their own travels. Depending on which aunt had the time to cart us around, we travelled across the Awadh belt to meet other relatives. Most often we were in the charge of my aunt, Suraiya Phupi, but occasionally tagged along whenever my grandmother Atia (whom we called Ammajaan), felt inclined to drop in on a particular cousin, often during weddings or births. I remember journeys to Kanpur, Unnao, Faizabad, Aligarh, and most frequently to Mustafabad, the ancestral family home in Rae Bareli. We learnt, through these journeys, to sleep out in the open in courtyards and on rooftops, use very basic toilets and along the way, encountered all sorts of distant cousins from the mofussils—uncles and aunts, some forgotten, others utterly memorable characters who can only thrive in small towns.

If Moharram fell during the summer holidays, then that was probably the most heightened 'Muslim' religious-cultural experience I was regularly exposed to. The family would wear black and attend gatherings known as majlis, where tales of the tragedy of Karbala—when members of the Prophet's family were brutally slain in a battle for control of the Muslim world— would be recited in dramatic poetry form or sung in the form of a lament. There would be weeping and beating of the chest and I remember complaining to my grandmother that I did not like the fact that women and girls had to sit behind a curtain in an uncomfortable spot while the men had the best seats and could see the speakers! As a little girl, I was often indulged and allowed to sit with an uncle in the men's section at family majlis. I was also struck by the fact that my aunts looked so cheerful after their bout of weeping and I suspect that was because of the cultural content—perhaps a great identification with the family of the Prophet—mixed with the catharsis that socially endorsed weeping performs for the human mind.

I vividly remember the Moharram in Mustafabad when I first saw the more dramatic public self-flagellation. Villagers in a procession were beating themselves with chains and hitting their heads with blunt knives, blood streaming down their faces. Then one day, a coal pit was dug in the family courtyard in Mustafabad; the embers lit, the villagers walked on coal. Members of my family stood and watched while this display took place. I remember thinking even then that it was bizarre that people should watch like the masters of ceremony, while others walked on hot coal. Some years ago, I read about a high cleric from Iran who visited Lucknow and said that the more extreme form of mattam (mourning through beating and cutting oneself) was not desirable. I was most amused to read that the Shia clerics of the Awadh region had protested against this statement.

Years ago, I internalized the message that religion can create some of the highest forms of cultural expression such as the epic Urdu poetry that describes the events at Karbala. But it can also spawn practices that must look retrograde to the modern eye. I believe that, in the Indian subcontinent, Moharram practices are more extreme than in West Asia because of local influences. So what did I take away from my summer holidays in Uttar Pradesh? Even with my half-baked Urdu, I can respond to and recognize a marsiya being recited, but that, too, did not determine any sense of religious identity. In my family, we were encouraged to see it all as a cultural experience, not a matter of faith. Religion, after all, is the opium of the masses.

My Ammajaan, now in her nineties, is still a force in the clan and, every Moharram, travels from Lucknow to Mustafabad, where she also runs a small school attached to the joint family property. Some years ago, she wrote an Urdu book on the epic poetry of Mir Anees, the nineteenth-century wordsmith born in Faizabad who described the events of Karbala with great beauty, drama and emotion. Each time she is in Delhi and visits my home, my grandmother leaves behind a verse in beautifully written Urdu about me, my daughter Sara, or a blessing for an event in our home. She says her prayers and always observes Moharram but is, in every sense, a complete liberal, who celebrates culture but is very dismissive of any intolerance or fundamentalism. Now that her hearing has become poor, it is more prudent to let her talk; she still has so much to say and delights in visiting or being visited by her many relatives.

However, back home in Delhi and at the head of the Christian wing of the family, my redoubtable Naani, underwent a transformation in the opposite direction. As she grew older, her world divided quite definitely into good and evil. Good were those who had seen the light of Jesus; the rest of us sinners were under Satan's evil sway. That, it appeared, was the central tenet on which her faith rested, and with somewhat frightening ferocity she set out to save our souls so that we do not burn in hell. My grandmother was an extraordinary woman. Just as she had shown great character in rebuilding her life, she now wanted to save her family from certain damnation. She was a tiny woman but was remarkably good at getting permissions from the Municipal Corporation of Delhi, land from the government for her schools and generally coaxing her way through the system. In her simple saris, this short woman was well-known in the neighbourhood. I remember the local taxi stand just had to be told we were calling from the home of Mrs Nathaniel and they would say 'Mataji ka ghar?' and take us wherever we wanted to go without question.

'Mataji' had by then become one of the pivots for Pentecostal Church activity in Delhi. She became a standard bearer for the Pentecostals and her home was the first stop for visiting foreign missionaries before they set off for the interiors to save the poor souls who probably had no idea they were going to be threatened with Hell and Damnation unless they saw the Light. Naani would take off for these missions with Sister Alice and Pastor George, and came back with tales of miracle healing:'Hallelujah, Praise the Lord. Dhanu's body was covered in scabs but they have disappeared with the light of Jesus. Oh praise Jesus, praise the Lord.' She would gather in her room with her various brothers and sisters (mostly Indians) and they would hold hands, weep in prayer and talk in various tongues. Once a week, there was a prayer meeting in her drawing room where people would clap and sing enthusiastically and recite a long emotional prayer. The songs were mostly in Hindi about the wonders of Yeshu Masih (Jesus Christ). Sometimes, the Americans would arrive. Most of them were middle-aged, church-going folk but there were some youngsters who'd landed in India because Jesus had saved them from drug addiction or domestic abuse.

There were three years of high school and college when I lived with Naani as my family had shifted to South India. She bluntly—and often—told me that I would burn in hell. In those days, I sometimes met her two sisters as well. Nancy, a principal of an excellent school in Rajasthan for several years came less frequently. But Pansy Aunty was a fixture at Naani's house after the death of her doctor husband. The old lady would sit beside her carrom board for hours, waiting for someone to play with her. Unlike Naani, who was out there saving the world, helping her daughters and running her schools, Pansy Aunty had nothing to do but kill time. I remember I once asked her what would happen to me when I went to hell. Pat came the reply: 'There will be burning coals under your feet, but when you jump up in pain, someone will hit you on the head with a bat so you will touch the coal again and jump again and be stuck in an endless cycle as hell is eternal and there is no escape from it as you can't die!'

Naani never painted such a vivid picture of hell though she spoke of Satan often. By then she was convinced that all her daughters and grandchildren would not enter the pearly gates of heaven as none had followed her faith. Two of my aunts had married Syrian Christians, two had wed Hindus, and my father was a Muslim, although I must say he tried his best to be enthusiastic about his mother-in-law's orientation by loudly proclaiming 'Praise the Lord!' every time he saw her. For some years, 'Praise the Lord' became a greeting in our home.

Naani was a remarkable woman who helped her daughters whenever they needed it. She bailed out my mother both in cash and kind on innumerable occasions. Because she realized that her daughter was trying to raise two kids on the salary of a reporter who seemed blow up all his meagre earnings on the Press Club and yet have an endless stream of relatives who landed up in their home, Naani gave my mother one of her schools and that was the bedrock on which we became somewhat financially stable. As children, we all adored her and I remember how, particularly during the Christmas vacations, all her daughters with their offspring would gather and there would be one long celebration in Naani's house.

But intolerance is a strain on the human spirit. Little kindnesses are lost in the idea of good and bad, absolute or nothing. As Naani began to judge and condemn too harshly, I remember beginning to avoid her. I suspect this also happened with her daughters and other grandchildren. In a sense, the bonds that were made in that home under the Christmas tree of an adored grandmother began to break. Hectoring and judging damages the vulnerable and takes the joy out of the moment, as someone is scared of having a finger pointed at them, another is nervously trying to make light of the matter. When she was the expansive grandmother, we were all there; when the narrow vision prevailed, we all scattered. My Naani the fanatic is now under the earth and if her vision of heaven and hell did hold up, then she is definitely one of the great characters in her blessed Kingdom of God.

In Good Faith

What I did understand from this experience is that, for those of us who do not expect to be transported to Jannat (Paradise) or Heaven, for those of us who want to keep our humanity alive but still seek spirituality, the answers must lie in a tradition that operates on the idea of compassion and accommodation. I have travelled to shrines across India but have ironically, found a few moments of peace at a dargah just a five-minute walk away from my home in Mehrauli, Delhi. It is the oldest dargah in Delhi of Qutubuddin Bakhtiar Kaki, the spiritual successor of Moinuddin Chishti of Ajmer. Bakhtiar Kaki's most famous follower was Baba Farid, who in turn became the teacher of Delhi's most famous Sufi saint, Nizamuddin Auliya, who gave spiritual guidance to the incredible Amir Khusro—musician, scholar, poet and the father of qawwali. Amir Khusro wrote in Persian and Hindavi, and played a seminal role in the evolution of language in the subcontinent. The Sufis of the Chishti order and Amir Khusro have shaped the way we are, the music we hear, the words we use, the non-doctrinaire approach to the divine.

It is the familiar qawwalis and the simplicity of the form that draws me to the dargah near my home on the occasional weekend. I have never delved into any complex prayer or practice. I just raise my hands and say thanks for what I have, pray for the people I care about; sometimes I tie a thread and ask for a boon, I offer flowers and incense sticks and on the way out, I distribute money to the needy. Sometimes the qawwals sing really well and I can hear their voices rising as I walk out. My daughter Sara, too, has come with me on occasion and I hope that she will take with her the message that the best prayer is not ritual but asking for others.

Today I must accept that, somewhere along the journey, I was boxed into being a Muslim. It happened for the first time when I was about twelve years old and went to attend a birthday party at the home of the Aggarwal brothers. When she was asking the children's names, their mother stopped when she heard mine. 'Tum hamare me se nahin ho (you are not one of us),' she said. I remember feeling strange and unclean. What did she mean, I wondered? Was it because we did not have pujas in our home or organize all-night jagrans as some of my friends did? I really resented that lady and avoided that home in the future.

The third cultural element that came into the Muslim-Christian potpourri was my exposure to a traditional Bengali Hindu background when I lived in Calcutta (now Kolkata) with my former husband, Prashun, and worked with the *Telegraph*. Calcutta was a larger-than-life experience—the friends, the addas, the Anandabazaar office on Prafulla Sarkar Street, the trams, the restaurants on Park Street, the sheer chaos of the place. Along the way I also became an insider in a Hindu home. There was elaborate puja at home in Calcutta and an introduction to the great public festivals of Bengal. There is nothing in North India that parallels the sheer colour, scale and sounds of the pujas of Bengal. If the Moharram observances of Awadh were a combination of the influence of faith and an evolved cultural and linguistic tradition, and the conversion drive of Christian missionaries driven by blind belief in one 'superior' God, the pujas of Bengal seemed like a part of a rather fantastic world where commerce mixed with religion and the whole State had a huge noisy party.

I absolutely loved it and visited pandal after pandal, mesmerized by the slow build-up and then the sheer abandonment of the dhunuchi naach performed in front of idols of Durga. I remember a train ride in Bengal with a compartment full of dhaakis travelling to Calcutta for the pujas. It was a dhak-a-dhak ride, quite memorable. But Calcutta in the late 1980s was still a city where the length of the power cuts was a topic of discussion, as the revolution of the communists had come and created its own hierarchies and disappointed in the world of ideas, leaving its citizens with nothing else to talk about. Mandal and mandir were beginning to change politics in the north but nothing was happening in Bengal.

By the time I returned to Delhi, I was deeply interested in the issues of religion, cultural forms and evolutions of identity, particularly as Indian politics was being reshaped on old fault lines, asserting a certain idea of the Hindu, promoting a certain stereotype of the Muslim. The real impetus to take on this work came from the almost desperate need to do something to combat the arguments of the fundamentalists. A property broker in South Delhi made it very clear to me that I was a Muslim and as far as the landlords of Delhi were concerned, no one liked to give their houses to Muslims. 'Madam, why don't you use your married name? South Indians and Bengalis are popular tenants.' Impressed by the broker's pragmatism, I decided to heed his advice and never revealed my real name while house-hunting in Delhi in those days.

Then in 1987, riots broke out in Meerut and since I didn't have a job then, I tagged along with Prashun, who was sent to cover them as a reporter with *The Indian Express* (Delhi edition). The experience shaped the way I thought and reacted from then on.

Meerut was already under curfew and an army convoy was patrolling the main street. On one side of the road was a middle-class Hindu neighbourhood, on the other side, a small Muslim mohalla known as Hashimpura. The police warned us against going to the Muslim area as 'they are all Pakistanis there and ready to shoot any outsiders'. The Hindus had set up vigilance committees to patrol and rebuff the Muslims who, they said, may come 'to take revenge and rape our daughters'.

On the second day, we gave our minders the slip and entered the streets of Hashimpura. There were bullet marks all over the walls as if someone had just fired at random. Terrified people were looking out of their homes. Only women and children were left; the men had been bundled up and taken away by the police (some days later, forty-two bodies were found floating down a canal). There was no food, and water had run out. The police had brutalized these people while telling the locals to guard against them. When Prashun returned to Delhi and filed the story, it was not carried by his editor who later became a BJP MP. Some days later, the *Times of India* broke the story about the Hashimpura massacre.

That was an age when the towns of Uttar Pradesh were being lit by communal fires, one after another. Some time in the mid to late 1980s, my father made a small series for Doordarshan titled 'Mera Bharat'—brief fillers on India's composite culture. It was the root of an idea that I would later pursue and examine more thoroughly, often challenging the romantic and simplistic approach to such traditions. My journey began some years later in the backdrop of the Ram Janmabhoomi movement and the consequent destruction of the Babri Masjid that seemed designed to change the nature of the Indian republic from a secular entity to one where the rights of the Hindu majority would be paramount. As India seemed consumed by Hindu-Muslim tension, many of us were scared and worried. The Right-wing BJP had announced its arrival on the national stage, and they were now a force to reckon with in Uttar Pradesh. For the first time, we were frightened. The Babri shrine was located in the northern town of Ayodhya, near Faizabad, where I have relatives and is a few hours' drive from our village home in Mustafabad that my grandmother still tries to preserve. In 1991, I remember my grandfather removing his name plate from the small legal practice he had run for years in Lucknow. His sudden decline in health began at that time and he passed away a year later. In Delhi too, the atmosphere changed. I was once told at a party by a public school educated man that 'you Muslims should know your place in India.' A reporter from a leading daily actually visited us to ask how a Hindu-Muslim marriage survived in these times, the question being, 'Do you fight over the Babri Masjid?'

One can hardly respond to such ugly questions and absurd positions, but I believed I could—and should—do something about it. After the demolition of the Babri Masjid on 6 December 1992, I quit my job as a sub-editor in a newsmagazine, got some minimal financial support from the late Professor Rasheeduddin Khan of the Jawaharlal Nehru University (who went on to head the Centre for Federal Studies at Jamia Hamdard University), worked out an arrangement to write a fortnightly column in the Sunday edition of *The Indian Express*, and set off on a journey across India to locate individuals, communities, shrines and traditions that represented some sort of unity as opposed to the divisions I then saw around me. Prashun, still a good friend, often accompanied me on these trips and for two years we travelled almost non-stop. I wrote a regular column in the Sunday edition of *The Indian Express* on my discoveries and those clippings form the archival material for this work. I also kept many notebooks with interviews, some day planning to make sense of the incredible things we saw, the people we met. I zigzagged across India in trains, across states in buses and, in some instances, reached the final destination in a village by bullock cart or on foot. When I stopped and resumed regular work as a journalist, many people would ask me why those articles were never compiled in the form of a book. I never had a good answer.

The truth was that, somewhere along the way, I had also begun to doubt the work itself. That's why it took me so long to give it serious shape. Having collected the material over several years, I became a non-believer. Did it really matter that we have a composite culture when fundamentalism is increasing and we are headed for more hatred between communities? Was it just some romantic notion of an age gone by? There were so many questions I asked myself. Over a decade spent covering national politics also did not help, as a political journalist is also trained to be a professional cynic.

But somewhere down the line, I knew I had to keep some idealism alive. Over the years, I would periodically return to this project that, in some sense, represented an India I would like to believe in, a culture I wanted to survive. I struggled with my own scepticism about it being categorised as 'romantic mush' to deem that it was worth my while and indeed, a valuable contribution to put down all the material I had collected and knock it into some sort of a sensible shape.

This is my offering in an age when Hindu majoritarism is always raising its ugly head, when Islamic puritanism is on the rise across the globe, and when issues of identity still determine our politics.

THE BEGINNING

In the period between the beginning and end of this project, I have had the benefit of hindsight, accumulated wisdom, and a greater ability to see life in shades of grey, as opposed to the black and white of youth. For this work, some of my old articles have been carried in part in some of the chapters but most have been rewritten and updated. Fresh pieces have been added. Moreover, my perspectives have changed since the time the project began. I have spent nearly eleven years covering the BJP—its emergence, consolidation and subsequent electoral defeat. Today, as the political editor of *Outlook* magazine, I write about the Congress and the UPA, the BJP and other national political trends, but my understanding of the Sangh Parivar and its affiliates has, in particular, shaped my understanding of identity issues.

In the current global environment, we are all familiar with the conservative/liberal debate and the idea of good Muslim/bad Muslim. Many of the traditions written about in this work would be haraam (blasphemous) according to the more conservative schools of Islam, such as the Deoband seminary. Although the conservative schools dominate institutions today and are increasingly patronized by government and quasi-State structures, the original Muslim experience in India was shaped by the liberal, eclectic Sufis and part of the social transformation triggered by them. I dwell on such processes and the Sufi-Bhakti amalgam later in the book. There are also chapters on popular culture promoted by Hindi cinema and Bollywood and on the personalities and traditions that have shaped the composite culture of Hindustani classical music and Hindi film music. I still have memories of Aseemun bai, who would sing lovely folk and classical songs in homes linked to the family in Awadh at every wedding, birth or celebration.

But let me add a caveat. In the course of working on this project, I have realized that there is a peculiar problem with the terms 'composite culture' or 'syncretistic traditions' in India. Everyone has their own expectations from them. On the one hand, there is the belittling of such traditions as impure practices that have corrupted the great religions. On the other, there is a glorification of our pluralism, and the expectation that it may somehow combat the growth of religious fundamentalism.

This work takes neither of these positions. It is a journalistic account of the existence of several fascinating traditions in our country at a time when the political landscape has been changing. This is by no means an academic work, although there are some references to local sources and works of research into specific regions or local traditions. But each chapter has the attention span of a journalist sniffing out a story and not the rigour of an academic.

But the sum of this work does give an insight into some of India's little-known cultural pockets and raises questions about how traditions come to exist; and conversely, how they can begin to die or change into something entirely different. There are several examples of Sufi shrines slowly transforming into something that belongs to the Hindu fold and shedding their so-called Muslim or Islamic forms. Sometimes (as we see in the State of Maharashtra), this trend is driven by aggressive Hindu politics, the creation of an entire narrative to prop up a certain mythology and also the desire to control a profitable place of worship.

Indeed, wherever there is religion, there is also thriving commerce. Having travelled across temples, dargahs and churches, both big and small, I have noticed that there is great financial impetus to both promoting a certain belief in the magical powers of the shrine and to control the revenue it generates. From the greedy pandas of the Jagannath temple at Puri to the rapacious caretakers of big Sufi centres, money is worshipped in the sacred landscape of India.

Then there is the question of who is a Muslim. Today, they are often viewed as the bearded and burqa-clad problem of modern India. But there is nothing uniform about Indian Muslims. This work also explores the several syncretic communities in the country, such as the Langas of Rajasthan on the western border and the Patachitra painters of Bengal in the east, who are grappling with their own unique existential crisis. All of them exist on the periphery of organized religions but they, too, are Muslims. Similarly, there are also stories here that fleetingly explore the Christian reality in our country.

There are great paradoxes everywhere, as the sacred and the profane, the profound and the shallow, exist side by side in our religious and cultural landscape. This work reflects my own prejudices and I take the liberty to come up with my own half-baked theories on popular culture and psychology. For instance, I would argue that all these little traditions may appear to be very folksy, unevolved, just about simple wish fulfilment, yet at the ground level they provide the counter to the fundamentalists of all religions. For instance, Brahmanical control over Hinduism has already been challenged by the evangelical telegurus. I would also argue that the great Hindu reverence for graves of dead saints of all religions (particularly the Sufis) and a belief in magical boons continues to challenge any orthodox construction of religion. Similarly, the Muslim orthodoxy, such as the conservative interpretation of Islam offered by the powerful Deoband seminary, also see these traditions as the great challenge to their vision of a uniform religious way of life that banishes any form of idol or grave worship.

But most Indians, regardless of their religious persuasion, are in search of a miracle. Because life is so hard that it is not the complex prayer that offers comfort but the belief in some simple magic.

YOUR GOD IS MY GOD
Nyaya village, Midnapore district, West Bengal

Imagine a person who is both a Hindu and a Muslim. Now imagine an entire village of such people. These are not delusional, split personalities or the residents of a crazy commune but an entire community that stands at the periphery of two religious identities. The Patachitra painters of West Bengal are quite unique in the Indian subcontinent. They struggle to maintain a fluid identity in the face of constant pressure to define themselves more rigidly, and are amongst the most extraordinary people I have met in the course of my travels.

It is their art form that is at the heart of the matter. The 'pat' or scroll painting is a unique art form found in Bengal and Orissa (now Odisha). While the Orissa scrolls are more classical and the painters all Hindus, in West Bengal it is a very folksy tradition and most of the surviving practitioners of the form are Muslims. The artist, referred to as a chitrakar or patua, paints images that tell a story in sequence. As the scroll is opened scene by scene, the artist accompanies it with a song narrative. Though there are a few scrolls about local Sufi saints and some that deal with contemporary issues such as the literacy drive, the bulk of the scrolls depict Hindu divinity. Episodes from the Ramayana and Mahabharata are brought to life by these moving pictures. The most popular subjects are the gods Rama, Krishna, Shiva, the Shakti figures revered in Bengal such as the goddesses Durga, Kali and Chandi, and prominent Hindu saint reformers like Chaitanya Mahaprabhu and Sri Ramakrishna. Most of the songs praising the gods have been handed down several generations.

Nyaya is a village of Patachitra artists who are described as 'Muslims' even though their identities are a cross-over. The village is one of the most prolific centres in Bengal of this dying form. The fifty-odd artiste families are indeed a curious community. They finalise marriages according to the Hindu calendar but the Muslim nikaah ceremony is solemnised by a Qazi. Funerals are conducted according to Islamic rites. While no woman has ever donned the veil (purdah), married women wear the vermilion mark (sindoor), a distinctly Hindu custom. And as far as festivals go, this artist community appears to have decided to make the best of both worlds. Eid is celebrated with as much enthusiasm as Durga puja.

Most curiously, all of them have two names, Hindu and Muslim. The Hindu name they claim is their professional name while their 'real' name is Muslim. All their last names are Chitrakar (artist). So Dukhoram Chitrakar's Muslim name is

Osman; Amar Chitrakar is also Omar, just as a woman artist, Rehima, goes by the name of Roopa Chitrakar.

Though the Patachitra art form is famous throughout Bengal, people have scant knowledge about this community of singer-painters. One would have imagined that they would be an anthropologist's delight, but research into the social origins of the community remains sketchy. One theory goes that they came from an untouchable Hindu caste that converted to Islam to escape social ostracism. The other theory is that they were a respectable caste of painters who gradually converted to Islam because many of their patrons were Muslim landlords (zamindars).

Either way, Bengal is that rare corner of India where the landlord has truly been vanquished after years of communist rule. So with their principal patrons gone, these artists struggle to keep their way of life alive. Some still muster the stamina to collect their little cloth bags full of scrolls and walk from village to village singing their songs, hoping to get a few rupees for the display of their colourful paintings, made from vegetable dyes. But the proliferation of television and cinema in the countryside has slowly been rendering them redundant as a form of local entertainment. Many of them now find it difficult to eke out a living from their art alone and also work as farm labourers during the harvesting season. Some have even started to make idols for the great festivals of Bengal such as Durga puja and Kali puja. There are a few who have also added snake charming to their incredible repertoire.

But this unique community has got an unexpected lease of life through the cultural festival circuit promoted by both the

State and Central governments in India since the mid-1980s. For all its apparent shallowness, the boutique culture developing in Indian metros, the idea of the ethnic chic, has helped keep body and soul together of several impoverished artisans and craftsmen. Some Patachitra painters have been beneficiaries of this trend. The West Bengal government now routinely sends a few for cultural festivals in the State, in other parts of India and even abroad. It is also not uncommon to see a scroll painting hanging on the walls of homes of the Bengali bhadralok in Kolkata. Several connoisseurs and collectors of folk art in Kolkata now routinely stock Patachitras and even offer to get some painted on demand for their customers. This is just the sort of push a small community needs to survive. This trend does, however, create a 'creamy layer' or elite within the community, the privileged few artists who often appear to corner all the benefits.

There is another facet and outcome of this new age patronage. Patachitra is traditionally a live art form, a living tradition. But the modern patrons are investing in the form without the content. The scrolls may survive but the delightful songs about the incredible adventures and dilemmas of the gods are being lost. Many painters now grumble that their children are losing interest and are keener on learning film songs and 'adhunik gaan' (modern Bengali pop). Even members of the community are uncertain about future generations remembering their songs. A prominent village resident, Sunder Chitrakar, asked me hopefully: 'Maybe some film song-writer will like our songs and adapt it for a mythological film or television series?'

The other great challenge these singer-painters face comes

from the Muslim clergy. I recorded a long interview with Dukhoram Chitrakar, a skilled artist who had made many rounds of the festival circuit over the years. He had analysed the patuas' position in the social hierarchy of Muslims: 'The mullahs don't like us. They tell other Muslims we are polluted. They say that by painting the gods we are indulging in idol worship. When we pay them a lot of money to solemnise a marriage or funeral they come and tell us to stop our haraam art and start saying our prayers five times a day.' Most other Muslims, except for those in the performing arts, do not inter-marry with the Patachitra painters.

In a way, these unusual people have been damned into continuing with their way of life. Roopa Chitrakar, with her flashing kohl-lined eyes, asked me defensively: 'Why should I not participate and sing in the pujas? I earn some money and have so much fun. I have also learnt to say the namaz.' Sunder Chitrakar got angry when questioned about his Muslim credentials: 'I have got tired of this. See, I have even grown a beard to show that I am a Muslim though I have not yet understood why Allah likes a beard. I am a Muslim, my children are Muslims and Allah knows it!'

So, do the Chitrakars live in a no man's land of religion? A senior official at the Midnapore district headquarters certainly believed so: 'They are the Muslim untouchables.' When I gently pointed out that, in principle, Islam does not accept castes, he laughed. 'Well, they are certainly not Hindu untouchables. We have too many of our own. Maybe, madam, you would be happy if, like Gandhi, we called those who are outcaste, the children of God.'

A MUSLIM GODDESS
Sundarbans, West Bengal

A journey into the Sundarbans is to venture into a terrain that lives by its own rules. Made up of little islands linked by waterways, they have no infrastructure for travellers who have to spend the night on boats or in the villages. There is a great stillness in the night at the edge of the land that disappears into the Bay of Bengal. There is the dark rustle of the forests, the gentle ripple in the water, the clouds moving swiftly across the moon and stars. There is a strange goddess who is believed to be the keeper of these parts. She is called Bonbibi and the locals say she is a Muslim goddess.

Even an 'impure' or ignorant Muslim knows there are no gods and goddesses in Islam. Idol worship is strictly banned. There is only Allah and his last prophet Mohammad and even he cannot be depicted in a picture or idol. Yet, the people of the Sundarbans have created a curious creature in the form of a Muslim goddess. In imagery and form, Bonbibi strongly resembles the several Shakti figures so popular in the State. Her devotees insist that she is not a metamorphosis of Goddess Durga or Kali, and are convinced that she is a Muslim.

Such a curious divinity could only have come into existence in an extraordinary landscape. Bonbibi's home is an unusual terrain: the Sundarbans, a vast tract of forest and swamp, is now divided between India and Bangladesh. A cluster of four hundred-odd islands linked by a network of waterways form the largest estuarine delta in the world. The Sundarbans is also the largest mangrove forest in the world, much of which is exclusive tiger territory. Even the tigers here are distinct from their brethren in other parts of India—they are smaller, accomplished swimmers, and most significantly, man-eaters. Studies have tried to determine whether the salinity of the water has caused the Sundarbans tigers to develop a taste for human beings, but no conclusive answers have been found. So lethal are these tigers that their appetite for man has led to numerous deaths every year. There is a village called Bagher Vidhava Gram, which literally translates into 'village of the tiger widows'—its inhabitants are all women whose husbands have had the misfortune of being eaten up.

Much of the region comes under Project Tiger where human habitations are banned. But there are several villages on the edge of the waterways and forests where a mixed population of Hindus and Muslim struggle to eke out a living through subsistence-level farming, a very basic form of fishing where villagers stand submerged in water for hours with their nets, woodcutting and honey collecting. The people are desperately poor and life in the delta is harsh. The rivers are constantly in flux and the islands change dramatically with the monsoons. Cultivated land is frequently flooded while the forest, the other source of income, presents many perils, particularly the tigers that claim at least fifty human lives every year.

In response to their environment, the locals, both Hindus and Muslims, have evolved a religion that is a curious mix of animism, the Hindu Shakti tradition and a typically Indian brand of Sufism, which is described by some scholars as the phenomena of 'Pirism' in Bengal. The Sufis are commonly described as the wandering Islamic mystics who spread Islam in much of the subcontinent. Pir is a Persian word that means 'spiritual guide'. In Bengal, it covers not only the Sufis but a range of holy men, some of whom appear to be completely mythical and represent various natural forces. All of them have been deified as Pirs.

The three most popular gods of the Sundarbans are Bonbibi, the Muslim forest goddess who is a Durga-like figure; a 'tiger god' named Dakshin Ray; and a legendary Pir named Ghazi Miyan. The legends of the three deities are inextricably woven together. In his landmark work, *The Islamic Syncretistic Tradition in Bengal*, historian Asim Roy, referring to the Sundarbans divided between India and Bangladesh, says that Hindu Ray-Mangal literature depicts Dakshin Ray as a Hindu chief who battled Ghazi Miyan, the Muslim, for control of the forest. He writes: 'An even battle, it was ended, we read, by a happy compromise based on territorial divisions dictated by God, appearing in a significant form, half Hindu and half Muslim.'

But the legend that I found most common in the district of 24 Parganas covering the Indian side of the Sundarbans was somewhat different. In this version, Dakshin Ray is a tiger god who wages a mighty battle with Bonbibi, the protector of humans. Finally, Ghazi Miyan is forced to intervene and he works out a compromise where the forest is equally divided between the two, human beings and tigers. The locals even perform an elaborate dance theatre based on this legend. It is a colourful event with villagers donning tiger masks, some dressing up as the goddess, and others putting on a very primitive beard and skullcap to depict Ghazi Miyan. This legend is enacted in a simple folk-theatre style to a riotous beating of drums and blowing of conch shells. The Bonbibi puja is a huge celebration in the forest and a delight for any visitor.

So who exactly is Bonbibi? She is definitely a less evolved Shakti deity, the female divine so worshipped across Bengal. Makeshift temples of Bonbibi line the edge of the forest and no local ventures inside without seeking her blessings. These temples are crude structures that usually have a single clay image of Bonbibi. The more elaborate temples are found in the villages. Here, the goddess stands alongside many consorts, which is usually a happy mix of Muslims and Hindus. Bonbibi also appears alongside the 'tiger god', Dakshin Ray, who also has to be appeased. At times she is merely standing beside him, in other temples she is vanquishing him, looking remarkably like Goddess Durga destroying the demon. The Bonbibi tradition clearly draws from animism, once popular across India but now found only in the Sundarbans. Animistic cults have died out because of large-scale deforestation across the country but survive in the Sundarbans because of the rare terrain. Equally popular in the region is the Mobrah Ghazi or

Ghazi Miyan tradition that survives not just in the forest area but throughout the 24 Parganas district. This tradition, too, originates in the need to seek protection from tigers, other animals and the vagaries of nature.

In the Sundarbans, Ghazi Miyan is worshipped alongside another figure called Kalu Ghazi and five Hindu deities. Some fakirs of the region, who claim descent from the Ghazi, accompany the locals into the forest where they perform an elaborate puja. The fakirs clear a space where they build seven small thatched huts in a single row. The first three huts are for the Hindu deities Jagabandhu (friend of the earth), Mahadeva (the destroyer) and Manasa (the snake goddess). The fourth hut houses Goddess Kali and her daughter Kalimaya while the fifth hut has two compartments: one for a goddess called Kamesvari and the other for Budi Thakurani, a local deity. The sixth hut is dedicated to Ghazi Miyan and his brother Kalu Ghazi and the seventh to Sawwal Ghazi, the son of Ghazi Miyan, and Ram Ghazi, the son of Kalu Ghazi. It's quite an intricate and elaborate pantheon.

After these preparations, offerings are made to all the deities and the fakir spends the whole night praying to Ghazi Miyan and his consorts to protect the party from tigers and other dangers. The legend of Ghazi Miyan is basically similar throughout the 24 Parganas, though there are some local variations in the names of his consorts. Santosh Chaudhary, a local teacher, says there have been attempts to create divisions and raise the issue of Bangladeshi refugees here. 'But here in the Sundarbans, who can tell a Muslim from a Hindu, a Bangladeshi from a Bengali? They are so alike that they have even entered into a joint enterprise over their gods. How can you separate the people when you can't separate their gods?'

Mohammad Sheikh is a woodcutter of great fame in the region. He has the scars of two tiger attacks: on his right shoulder and the back of his neck. This is the price he has paid for repeatedly venturing deep into tiger country in quest of the famed Sundarbans honey. As his name suggests, Mohammad Sheikh is a God-fearing Muslim. But he does not credit Allah for saving him from a gruesome death; it is the blessing of Bonbibi, he believes.

She does not appear to be doing a very good job of it, I suggest, what with so many humans becoming a meal for the beast each year. Wouldn't it be better to trust in Allah and his last prophet after whom you have been named? Mohammad Sheikh sees the world in black and white: 'Allah has too many human beings to deal with. Tigers are better left to Bonbibi.'

THE EKTARA AND A SONG
Kenduli, Bardhaman district, West Bengal

They epitomize the ultimate in liberation. A single string instrument in hand, they wander from village to town, singing of a love that does not accept boundaries and barriers. The Bauls of Bengal are another rare people who defy the notion of divisions. But first, a caveat about the landscape in which they operate. Few parts of India have such tortured histories as Bengal. It was here that the British first implemented their policy of divide and rule and some of the earliest recorded communal clashes took place in undivided Bengal. The region has undergone the trauma of not one but two partitions: the British-sponsored 1905 division and the 1947 Partition into West Bengal and East Pakistan, which eventually became the independent nation of Bangladesh.

That the Partition was a messy and imperfect arrangement is clear from the fact that a steady stream of Bangladesh refugees continue to enter India. And if it was designed to separate Muslims and Hindus, it has spectacularly failed to do so in Bengal. Muslims make up a quarter of West Bengal's population, one of the highest such ratios in India. Much of Kolkata's middle class is composed of Hindu refugees who abandoned their homes and lands in former East Pakistan. Logically, both in the city and the countryside, where pressure on land is intense, there is considerable scope to play on communal feelings.

Yet Bengal has remained relatively free of the communal virus. Part of the reason is the long spell of communist rule and the Left's horror of any sort of religious mobilisation. The other reason, some scholars argue, is because centuries of inter-community mingling have created a culture more defined by language than religion. Another possible reason, I believe, is the fact that the early authors of Islam in the region also cast their religion in a syncretistic mould. This, however, is a changing process as there have been attempts to create a more 'correct' Islamic consciousness and 'purify' the religion.

Yet there is no denying that the interaction between Hinduism and Islam has created several fascinating traditions in Bengal, particularly in the performing arts and crafts. Perhaps the best known, both in contemporary Bengal and in the rest of India, is that of the wandering Baul singers. The Bauls can be defined as an order of village singers drawn from both the Hindu and Muslim communities. Clad in flowing robes, strumming a single-stringed instrument called the ektara, they wander across the countryside singing of a universal God (there are also celebrity Bauls who wonder from concert to concert!). The Bauls stress the mystical concept of divine love and consider themselves a separate religious order. The great Vaishnav Bhakti reformer of Bengal, Chaitanya Mahaprabhu, has influenced the Bauls from the Hindu community. Those from the Muslim community are clearly influenced by Sufi mysticism. The Baul order as such is the result of a Bhakti-Sufi fusion.

The Bauls refuse to observe any of the conventions of formal religion and abhor all rituals. The outpouring of the heart through song and dancing in a state of ecstasy form their central religious activity. One can see the impact of Bengal's Vaishnavism, which uses music as a form of devotion, and the Sufi practice of sama (song and dance). The central religious belief of the Bauls is that God lies not in a temple or mosque but in the heart of man.

A typical Baul song, handed down by one of the better-known Baul singer-composers, Madan Baul, attacks both the formal religions:

> *The way to Thee has been blocked by both temple and mosque;*
> *I hear your call, my God, but I cannot proceed to you,*
> *as the guru and murshid stop me.*
> *The door is fastened with many locks,*
> *Quran, Puran, Tashib and Mala.*
> *The path of initiation is the main problem;*
> *afflicted as he is, Madan dies crying.*

The Bauls have given Bengal some of its most beautiful songs. Even Bengal's great poet and Nobel Laureate Rabindranath Tagore, credits many of the tunes of 'Rabindra Sangeet'—the music form he created—to these wandering minstrels. Tagore has said that he had once chanced to hear a song from a beggar of the Baul sect. 'What struck me in this simple song was a religious expression that was neither grossly concrete and full of crude detail, nor metaphysical in its rarefied transcendentalism.' He has, since then, been known to be inspired by the Baul singers and has used many of their tunes for his songs.

Though the word Baul covers members of all communities, the average Bengali refers to those of Muslim origin, distinguished by flowing beards and black or patchwork robes, as fakirs. The greatest Baul composer was Lalan fakir, and his entire body of work is simply referred to as Lalan gaan (Lalan's songs). Orange is the colour preferred by the Bauls of Hindu origin. But Hindu or Muslim, the Bauls sing the same songs and have the same literature and philosophy.

The earliest Bauls have been traced to Nadia district around sixteen centuries ago. Some historians believe that the revival of Brahminism among the Vaishnavs in the latter part of the sixteenth century resulted in many followers of Chaitanya Mahaprabhu leaving the Bhakti order and settling for the mysticism of the Bauls. Similarly, influenced by the Sufi tradition of seeking a personal equation with God, many Muslims also took to the itinerant lifestyle of the Bauls.

Through the year, several Baul melas (fairs) are held across Bengal. The largest is the Jaydev Kenduli Mela on the banks of the river Ajay in Bardhaman district. Kenduli is the birthplace of Jaydev, author of the *Geet Govinda*, the wonderful collection of devotional songs. In mid-January every year, thousands pour into this tiny village for three days of non-stop music by the Bauls. The fair is an unforgettable experience as the Bauls transport you to their simple world through their songs.

A fakir sings: After much deliberation, I see all is I,
I am he, I am he.
Ah me, people speak ill of me.
From I, Allah and his apostles come;
everything comes from I.
For whosoever knows himself, knows God.

It is not hard to understand why religious puritans would dislike the Bauls. Though by and large they are left alone, there have been some reports of attacks on them in the districts of Nadia and Murshidabad on the Bangladesh border. The brunt has been borne by the Muslim fakirs. Take the case of Sadar fakir of Kurchaidanga, a village in Nadia. His life revolved round his ektara and the songs that debunked religion. 'The search for Allah and the gods is futile,' Sadar would sing. 'Salvation lies in a universal love for mankind.' But the local Muslim clergymen did not agree. In September 1996, they called a religious congregation and declared Sadar a kafir (non-believer). That did not really trouble Sadar who had never pretended to be a believer. But then his land was forcibly cropped, his home ransacked and he was sternly forbidden from singing within the village boundaries. 'My soul was murdered,' he lamented.

Similar treatment was meted out to Omar Shah, the fakir of Alinagar village in Nadia district. The village elders called a meeting and charged him with sacrilege; he was dragged out of his home and his beard shaved. His neighbours were barred from socializing with him. His son moved out of the family home to escape the clergymen's wrath; even worse, he was told that he should not allow his own son to come near him. This sort of social boycott was also imposed on some Bauls in the neighbouring Murshidabad district. In 1997, ten fakirs of Dharampur village were declared social outcastes. At that time, Kazem Sheikh, one of those ostracized, had said: 'Our only fault is that we believe we are first human beings. Being Hindus or Muslims is only incidental.' Hindu Bauls also have to confront increased religious polarisation. When Gauranga Hazra of the Hindu dominated Beldanga village in Murshidabad took on a Muslim fakir as his guru, he was beaten up, his hut burnt down and he was socially boycotted.

Such incidents are nasty but they still remain a flash in the pan. Shakti Nath Jha, president of an umbrella organization of the Bauls says that, 'The Hindu bigots and Muslim fanatics feed on each other. Sometimes we come in the way and become targets. But we can organize ourselves to oppose them as the people of Bengal are with us because our songs are part of their lives.'

The Bauls remain an extraordinary order of village singers. They represent the essential unity of Bengali people, Hindu or Muslim, Indian or Bangladeshi.

THE PUJARI OF THE PIR
Kolkata, West Bengal

There are individuals who sometimes step out to create their own composite religious space. Years ago I met Biman Bhattacharya, a priest at the famous Kali temple at Kalighat, Kolkata. Even though he was at the Kalibari temple every day, he was equally devoted to Manickpir, one of the many Islamic saints worshipped throughout Bengal. Forty-five years ago, Bhattacharya built a small shrine dedicated to this Pir in Topsia, a Muslim dominated locality in South Kolkata. For years he visited the tiny mazhaar every Thursday, performed pujas at the saint's grave and then distributed 'prasad' amongst the local Muslims of the area.

Bhattacharya never saw any contradiction in being a worshipper of both Kalimata and Manickpir. 'They both have the power to perform miracles and grant boons,' he told me. His reason for building a shrine in Topsia is because he claimed that the Pir helped him out of trouble many years ago and continues to bless him again and again. He answered my queries on his dual faith by saying: 'My worshipping Manickpir does not stop me from being a good Hindu. I may be a Brahmin priest but my religion has taught me respect for all religions. Besides, throughout Bengal you will find Hindus praying at dargahs and mazhaars. I am not unique in my beliefs.' The last time I visited Kolkata I could not find Bhattacharya at the Kali temple and was told he was away because of poor health. But I remember him well and am told that the shrine to Manickpir still survives.

Bhattacharya was right in saying he was not unique. In Bengal, the term 'Pir' applies not only to historical saints and holy men but even to some mythical divinities who are worshipped as saints. In different parts of India, there are different local factors that contribute to the spread of Islam. In Bengal, the wandering Sufis played a particular role in the spread of agriculture. Historians say they won patrons among the local zamindars who donated tracts of land to these Pirs who then acted as community leaders and helped villagers clear land for cultivation. The religious message they carried was simple: belief in one God and the equality of men. The spread of Islam in Bengal (including Bangladesh) was, therefore, intrinsically linked to the clearing of land. This is possibly the reason for Bengal being that rare part of the country where Muslims are found to be in greater numbers in the countryside than in the cities. Statistics reveal that, while Muslims elsewhere in India tend to be clustered in urban centres, the Bengali Muslim is overwhelmingly rural.

The role of the wandering Pir is, therefore, central to Islam in Bengal. And the religious message of these Pirs was no dogmatic Islam but a flexible faith that accommodated many of the pre-Islamic beliefs of the converts. It was only after the reformist campaigns of the early nineteenth century that the fundamentalist fringe, with their stress on 'pure' Islamic practices, emerged amongst the Muslims of Bengal. But Islamic orthodoxy has never been able to throttle the syncretic tradition in Bengal. However, today, a growing consciousness among Muslims to stress their distinctiveness is being noticed.

Yet the dargahs and mazhaars remain central to Muslim faith in Bengal. Whenever Pirs died, their benefactors and followers would construct mazhaars over their graves. In the course of time, these tombs were credited with miraculous powers and the dead Pir came to be worshipped like a religious deity. To date, it is the mazhaar and not the masjid that exerts the maximum pull on the Muslim masses in the Bengal countryside. These mazhaars have also played a role in fostering healthy inter-community relations as, in many instances, Hindus such as the priest from the Kali temple are as involved as the Muslims in keeping alive the tradition of a particular Pir.

But the Manickpir he worships falls in the range of fictitious (as opposed to historical) Pirs. Presumably, the fictitious Pirs represent pre-Islamic local divinities that have been transformed into Pirs. Small shrines to Manickpir are found throughout Bengal and he is undoubtedly one of the most popular fictitious Pirs in the State. Maniktala in North Kolkata is named after this Pir and fairs and melas are held in his honour throughout the year in the countryside. He is considered the guardian of wealth, prosperity, health and fertility. It is difficult to trace the origins of the Manickpir cult though there are numerous folk ballads, songs and legends about the saint himself. We can simply surmise that this cult belongs neither to pure Islam nor Hinduism and is the result of their fusion at the level of popular religion.

EXPUNGING ISLAM
Thane, Maharashtra

Traditions are as fragile as the human condition. Till now we have been examining lovely little traditions, people and shrines that represent a certain fusion and the willingness to think outside the narrow confines of religious and social norms. In the course of this journey I found a most dramatic change between the east and the west, more specifically between Bengal and Maharashtra. If Bengal has witnessed relative communal peace through history, Maharashtra has, more often than not, served as a laboratory for Hindutva. It is the State where the RSS was founded, the State that produced Nathuram Godse (the assassin of Mahatma Gandhi) from the Hindu Mahasabha, and in the modern age is the home of the Shiv Sena, a political party known for the most lumpen brand of Hindu extremism. It is no coincidence that the repercussions of the demolition of the Babri Masjid were first felt in Mumbai—the industrial heart of India and capital of

Maharashtra—in the most vicious anti-Muslim violence seen since the Partition. Consequently, the State has been the target of bomb blasts presumed to be at the hands of Muslim extremists while recent investigations have shown a small cult of Hindu terrorists also making towns like Malegaon in Maharashtra their focus.

It is in the midst of such an atmosphere that traditions are given a hard communal edge. Processes have been underway in the State to divest certain Sufi shrines of their Islamic identity and include the 'divinities' as part of Maharashtra's Hindu pantheon. This has often led to communal tension at shrines that were once a symbol of religious harmony. Take the saga of the popular Haji Malang shrine in Thane, near Mumbai. As the name Haji (someone who has completed the Haj pilgrimage to Mecca) suggests, this is a shrine built up around the grave of a Sufi saint. District records from Thane note that people of all communities have paid homage at the shrine during the annual Urs festival. District records also describe Haji Malang Baba as a Sufi saint from Arabia who settled in the region and attracted many followers, both Hindus and Muslims. His closest disciple was a Hindu princess who is also buried in the complex. There appears to be no historical confusion that this is a dargah. One unusual feature is that the management of the dargah has been in the hands of a Hindu family for several generations—it is believed that this tradition was established by the Hindu princess.

In February 1993, on the heels of the Babri Masjid demolition and the Mumbai riots, the local Shiv Sena unit suddenly claimed that Haji Malang was not a mausoleum of a

Muslim Sufi but a tomb of a Hindu godman. They therefore demanded that the name should be changed from Haji Malang to Sri Malang. It was an outrageous claim but at that time the Sena had the muscle to make it. On visiting Haji Malang, I soon realised that greed also played a part in the Sena's religious zeal; it was keen to corner some of the huge profits the shrine made. The Sena men claimed to have 'discovered' a bell, a swastika and a trishul, all overtly Hindu symbols, within the shrine. Hence they demanded it should be treated as a temple. The Sena even came up with a name for the Hindu saint they claimed was buried in the complex— Shri Machhindarnath.

But they ran up against opposition, not just from the Muslim ranks (although at that point Muslims in the region were too terrified to oppose the Sena) but also from the Brahmin family that had been the traditional caretakers of the shrine. Kashinath Gopal Ketkar had no doubts about what sort of shrine he managed: 'There is no doubt that this is a dargah. My forefathers told me that the Baba Malang respected all faiths and that is why we do not have any prescribed rituals at the shrine. He wanted his resting place to be a symbol of all religions.'

Besides, Ketkar pointed out that further proof of this being a Sufi shrine is the fact that the main festival has always taken place during the annual 'Urs' (death anniversary) when mullahs arrive to assist in the rituals, even as Hindu minstrels sing songs in praise of the saint. The frescoes and motifs within the shrine were also distinctly Islamic in character.

Why then, did the Sena make such an extraordinary claim, with its leader Bal Thackeray even telling his cadres to march and 'liberate' the shrine? The Sena's desire to extend its influence over a wealthy and popular place of worship could be part of the reason. The more insidious and dangerous motive could, however, be a determination to deny the Muslim roots of a shrine venerated by thousands of Maharashtrian Hindus.

Although the Sena has not succeeded in taking over the shrine, they have destroyed its value as a symbol of inter-religious harmony. Since 1993, Haji Malang has been a disputed shrine, a source of protracted communal tension. Now every year, during the annual festival, a huge police force is deployed to stop any Hindu-Muslim skirmish. It has become a monument to the depressing politics and divisions of contemporary India.

We cannot fight the battles over the identity and origins of certain shrines on the basis of historical evidence alone. The popular imagination, the popular tales, the local belief systems play a big role in keeping alive traditions we may view as composite. These traditions cannot be seen as static at any point of time.

A MAZHAAR BECOMES A MANDIR
Madhi village, Ahmadnagar, Maharashtra

The metamorphosis of a mazhaar (Sufi shrine) into a mandir (temple) is a uniquely Indian phenomenon. The Haji Malang project is yet to be completed. But a similar process appears to have succeeded in another popular shrine in Madhi village of Ahmadnagar district. It is a shrine known locally as Kanifnath Kanobha, and has a distinctly rural flavour. Which is why the Hindu-Muslim tug of war, usually an urban phenomena, is more worrying here.

The shrine was originally a mazhaar. Although there is no scholarly study of the shrine, it does find a mention in the *Ahmadnagar District Gazetteer* compiled by the British: 'Madhi is a noted place of pilgrimage with a shrine or a dargah of the Musalman-Hindu saint Shah Ramzan Mahi Savar or Kanobha. He is believed to have come to the region in 1350 where he was converted to Islam by one Sadat Ali. After travelling for some years, he came to Madhi in 1380 and died here at the age of ninety.' The saint is believed to have exercised miraculous powers and the *Gazetteer* notes that 'his Musalman name is said to be derived from his having crossed the river Godavari mounted on [the] large fish, Mahi Savar.'

One of the largest rural fairs of Maharashtra takes place during the annual festival of the Madhi shrine. The date—the fifth of Phagun (March-April)—is determined by the Hindu calendar. There are some local Muslims who still come to worship and take part in the festivities. But the bulk of the two hundred thousand devotees are from the lower Hindu castes and tribes. They camp at the shrine for fifteen days and each caste and tribe holds a separate panchayat (conference) where issues ranging from literacy, family planning and village disputes to inter-caste rivalries are debated. It is a fascinating gathering of rural folk from across the State.

The regular devotees and village folk who gather here do not really seem engaged in the disputes arising from identity politics but the present caretakers of the shrine are deeply aware of religious symbolism. As far as they see it, this shrine now belongs to Hindus. There is a conscious effort to denude the shrine of its Islamic symbols and motifs.

Some of the local Muslims complain that the shrine has been completely taken over by loyalists of the Shiv Sena, who are dishonouring the memory of Shah Ramzan. Other Muslim residents don't really care as they see this type of Sufi cult as being anathema to correct Islamic practice. The upshot is that most of the symbols at the shrine are now overtly Hindu. Outside the main structure housing the saint's grave, a huge trishul and a temple bell can be seen. Pictures of the Hindu gods Shiva and Ma Santoshi have been placed next to the grave, while images of a dozen odd Hindu divinities adorn the walls.

Except for the interred saint's grave itself, there is no trace of the shrine's Muslim origins in the main structure. There is a smaller building opposite which houses the graves of the saint's close disciples. It has yet to be transformed into a temple and still looks like a dargah with a distinctly Islamic gumbaz (dome).

The priests at the shrine go to pains to deny any links with Sufi Islam. They insist that it is a temple of a Hindu saint called Kanifnath Kanobha. Local residents say that Hindu control over a profitable pilgrimage centre has been increasing since the Partition and has become nearly absolute since the ascendancy of the Shiv Sena. Only one Muslim is left in the fifteen-member management committee and all the caretakers who live within the shrine are Hindus. Two Muslim mullahs do, however, come to the shrine during the annual festival. They perform the Islamic rites while Hindu priests do puja.

At a superficial level, therefore, the shrine still remains a symbol of Hindu-Muslim synthesis. But it raises vital questions about the changing nature of both religions in the Indian subcontinent. The uniquely Indian Bhakti-Sufi fusion is what led to the establishment and popularity of shrines such as the Madhi dargah. But Islamic reform movements, the separatist politics that led to the Partition and Hindu fundamentalism have all taken their toll.

The saga of this little village shrine is also a living study of the inclusive polytheistic Hindu tradition, which, almost greedily, does not hesitate to adds gods upon gods to its pantheon.

A HINDU WARRIOR AND
A MUSLIM SAINT
Maharashtra

There are two historical figures from Maharashtra who have steadily captured the nation's imagination. The first is the seventeenth-century Maratha chieftain, Shivaji, whose battles against the Mughal rulers are the stuff of folklore across India. The second is a Muslim fakir who died as recently as 1918 in the little town of Shirdi in Maharashtra. Known simply as the Shirdi Sai Baba, he became a pan-India God-like figure in a remarkably short time and has been virtually incorporated into the Hindu pantheon. Both men are extraordinary figures, not so much because of the lives they led, but because of the impact their legends and myths have had on public imagination in contemporary India.

Shivaji is represented as a military hero, his adventures against the Mughal armies posited as a Hindu-Muslim battle. He cuts an appealing figure because he is the underdog, a

David-like figure up against the mighty Goliath of the Mughal Empire. The Shiv Sena takes its name from Shivaji and not the Hindu God, Shiva. Historians have long challenged the myths created around Shivaji by Hindu ideologues. They have argued that his fabled encounters with Mughal kings were a straightforward territorial contest and not the Hindu version of a holy war. Moreover, Shivaji's father, Shahaji Bhonsle served the Muslim Adil Shahi kings of Bijapur for years and was one of the kingdom's most powerful generals.

But what is less known is that Shivaji had deep links with the Sufi saints who were active in the region. If anything, it is this association that raises interesting questions and perhaps challenges the fundamentalists' appropriation of Shivaji as an anti-Muslim hero. Shivaji's grandfather, Maloji Bhonsle, had begun the family tradition of consulting Sufi saints. He had particular faith in a saint who lived near Ahmadnagar, named Shah Sharief, whose blessings he sought to have children. So when Maloji did eventually have two sons, he named them after the Sufi saint—Shahaji, who was Shivaji's father, and his uncle, Serfoji. And Shivaji himself was particularly close to a Sufi saint named Sayed Yaqub, whom he would often consult before launching a military campaign.

These are all historically recorded details, but what is startling is that unless one sets out to search for such information, it remains virtually unknown across India. These fascinating details came my way thanks to a chance meeting with Dr P. V. Ranade, former Head of the History Department of Marathwada University in Aurangabad. When we met in 1993 for the first time, Dr Ranade was despairing that even the so-called 'secular historians' have chosen to ignore some of these facts. In the political climate of Maharashtra, Shivaji was not open to historical scrutiny—many intellectuals, scholars and historians had been attacked for suggesting anything contrary to the popular myths prevalent in the State.

Dr Ranade cited several sources to maintain that the Sufis had struck deep roots in the Maharashtra hinterland. In a paper on the parallels between Sufism and Vedanta, he wrote: 'The spiritual authority of the Sufis extended to almost all the houses of the landed aristocracy. Shivaji's father and uncle carried the celebrated name of Shah Sharief, the Sufi saint of Ahmadnagar, on their person.' The Shah Sharief shrine still preserves the originals of a huge land grant made by Maloji.

Shivaji's grandfather had also gifted land to another prominent Sufi named Sheikh Mohammad, who set up base in Shrigonda, 70 kilometres from Ahmadnagar. There he wrote numerous works in Marathi such as *Pavan Vijay*, *Bhakti Bodh* and *Achar Bodh*. His landmark Marathi work, however, was the *Yoga Sangram*, which drew parallels between Sufism and Vedanta and freely combined the diction of Muslim and Hindu scriptures. Sheikh Mohammad's works were given pride of place by the Hindu Bhakti saints and are believed to have inspired Eknath, the greatest Bhakti figure from Maharashtra.

In an article titled 'Binocular Glossary of Vedanta and the Tasawuf of Sheikh Mohammad', Dr Ranade writes: 'Sheikh Mohammad did his job so very ably that his works were accorded almost a holy sanction in the Maharashtrian Warakari silsila. In fact, the poet Saint Samarth Ramdas, who is believed to have been the spiritual mentor of Shivaji, paid salutation to

Sheikh Mohammad in the following words: "Glory to Sheikh Mohammad, you have unfolded the mystery of the universe in such diction and style that it baffles the reason and logic of ordinary mortals... I will carry the sacred dust raised by your feet on my head."'

This marvellous confluence between Bhakti and Sufi is part of Maharashtra's heritage. And even today, it remains alive in parts of the State. At Sheikh Mohammad's dargah at Shrigonda, one of his followers, Sheikh Maqbool, still recites the *Yoga Sangram* daily before a village audience of both Hindus and Muslims. He recites in Marathi: 'The Vedas and Puranas tell us that he who respects the name of Hari will be blessed...' The namaz follows this extraordinary recitation.

There is, therefore, another side to Chhatrapati Shivaji, a narrative that has never been able to evolve or the story told. All of this must force us to confront the reality that history is often told in ways to confirm stereotypes and prejudices. This tendency gets sharpened when political mobilization depends on a particular tale being told in a certain way. At the Sheikh Mohammad dargah, they say that to equate the valiant Maratha chieftain with the Shiv Sena's doctrine of hatred is not only a distortion of history but is also a desecration of his memory. The fact that Shivaji fought numerous battles against rulers who happened to be Muslims does not mean that he despised Islam or the Muslim community, they say.

The State has some extraordinary examples of syncretic cultures, even as they are under assault from forces of the Right. In Daulatabad, at the samadhi of a Hindu saint known as Manpuri Baba, who is famous for having composed numerous bhajans, both Hindus and Muslims collect every Thursday night and sing these bhajans together. Among the bhajan singers is Maqsood Ali, who tells us about Manpuri Baba's friendship with a Sufi saint of neighbouring Aurangabad, Shah Nur Miyan. The legend goes, that on hearing of Shah Nur's death, Manpuri Baba also decided to give himself up to God. A picture of Shah Nur still hangs over the samadhi of Manpuri Baba. There are numerous other examples of the links between the Sufi and Bhakti saints of Maharashtra.

The integrative role of the saints and their dargah has, unfortunately, been undermined in the course of the twentieth century. Simultaneously, the fortunes of Right-wing Hindu groups have been on the ascendant. If Maharashtra is the home of Sheikh Mohammad and Sant Ramdas, it is also home to the Shiv Sena and the RSS, headquartered in Nagpur.

It is in this sort of landscape that the Sai Baba phenomenon took place, although the Shirdi Sai Baba is not merely a locally revered figure, but has become a national saint divinity. There are Sai Baba temples across the land, his posters and images adorn millions of homes, and thousands of Indians wear Sai Baba amulets and lockets. His shrine in Shirdi has become one of the richest pilgrimage spots in India, and certainly the most famous in Maharashtra. The Sai Baba of Puttaparthi in Andhra Pradesh, who recently passed away and had an impressive following of influential politicians and businessmen, had claimed to be a reincarnation of the Shirdi Sai Baba. Several mythological films have been made about the Shirdi Sai Baba and he is routinely depicted in Bollywood films as performing great miracles.

In Good Faith

What is curious about the Shirdi cult is that some of its most devout followers are also the authors of the Hindutva (Hindu Right) project. Many members of the RSS and BJP have images of the Shirdi Sai Baba in their homes. He looks like a typical Muslim fakir with a beard and a cloth tied over his head. But his followers see no contradiction between worshipping a so-called Muslim man while devising a political project that is designed to marginalize the community.

In a book titled *Sai Baba of Shirdi: A Unique Saint*, M. V. Kamath and V. B. Kher maintain that his origins remain unclear. In one part of the book they put forward the theory that he could have been a Brahmin and it was never conclusively proved that he was a Muslim. In the lore about Sai Baba, his devotees are divided on the issue of his origins. Some maintain he was not circumcised and hence not a Muslim, others say his ears were pierced and that was more common among Hindus. Today, the powerful and rich Sai Baba properties, trusts and buildings in Shirdi and across India, are a virtual industry. And while he is a great revered figure for Hindus, it is not so for Muslims, who do not include Sai Baba in the line of Sufi saints who are venerated across the subcontinent.

Yet we cannot overlook the fact that Sai Baba dressed like a fakir and lived in a rundown mosque in Shirdi. But he kept a fire going in the mosque and as his fame spread, devotees were allowed to blow conch shells and worship him in their own ways. In the end, what comes through is a fakir who had great respect for Hindu traditions. His most frequently uttered words were 'Allah Malik' (Allah is the Lord) but he also sang bhajans (devotional songs) in praise of the Hindu gods. It is said that at his behest, the locals decided to celebrate Urs (a Sufi celebration) and the Ram Navami festival on the same day. When the villagers collected money to repair the dilapidated mosque where the Sai Baba lived, he is believed to have insisted that all the local temples should first be repaired.

Kamath and Kher claim there is evidence that Sai Baba knew the Gita well and understood Hindu scriptures. B. V. Narasimha, founder president of the All India Sai Samaj and author of a four-volume biography of Sai Baba written in 1955, insists that the birth and parentage of Sai Baba are 'wrapped in mystery...we have not come across any person who has direct knowledge of them.' According to Kamath and Kher, Sai Baba discouraged questions on his parentage and gave mysterious and vague answers. The facts about him that are known are that he came to Shirdi between 1868 and 1872 and first lived on the village outskirts, then under a neem tree and finally moved into the dilapidated masjid. He collected alms and over the years also collected a band of devotees. At one point, a local Qazi opposed devotees worshipping him in the mosque. Soon after this, it was decided to hold the Urs and Ram Navami celebrations on the same day. As he grew older, he was credited with performing miracles and people began to travel to Shirdi in droves. In 1917, Congress leader and freedom fighter Bal Gangadhar Tilak visited Shirdi to meet him. A year later, in 1918, the Sai Baba passed away.

The huge shrine that has now come up at Shirdi largely functions as a temple but it does keep up traditions that represent the sort of Hindu-Muslim synthesis that Sai Baba propagated. A sacred fire believed to have been lit by him still burns in the mosque and every Thursday night, a colourful procession carries his picture from the village temple to the local mosque. There are several reasons why his cult has become so popular in such a short time, and one of the more fascinating arguments put forth is that he has been a particular favourite of the Bollywood film producers. Perhaps the many devotional songs in praise of Sai Baba, the film and television series about him, have all contributed to making this one of the most popular religious cults of contemporary India. That the origins lie in the saga of a fakir is significant.

Some RSS ideologues put an interesting spin on this and argue that they revere the Sai Baba because he represents their idea of an ideal Muslim. They see him as someone who does not condemn polytheisms but actively promotes it. As K. Govindacharya, RSS ideologue, told me: 'He is a bad Muslim but a good Hindu. He now belongs to us.' The RSS-Shiv Sena's high comfort levels with the Sai Baba tradition can also be deconstructed somewhat more cynically: the Sai Baba represents a Muslim who knows his place in a Hindu dominated society. He appeases the majority and does not stress on the distinctiveness of the minority.

THEY CRY FOR HUSSAIN
Andhra Pradesh

The phrase 'Hobson-Jobson' is described as 'an Anglo-Saxon version of the wailings of the Mohammedans as they beat their breasts in the processions of the Moharram and utter cries of "Ya Hussain!"'. If the British tongue could twist 'Ya Hussain, Ya Hussain' into Hobson-Jobson, small wonder then that the Indian love of revelry has transformed Moharram, a time of mourning for Shia Muslims, into a celebration in many parts of the country.

This is particularly seen in Andhra Pradesh, large parts of which were ruled by the Shia Qutb Shahi dynasty and later by the Asif Jahi Nizams who continued to patronize Shia institutions and placed many Shia Muslims in powerful positions. The result was that some Shia customs got absorbed into the indigenous culture and, in the process, Moharram was transformed into a sort of local folk celebration. This discovery was particularly fascinating for me given my exposure to Moharram during my childhood, the solemn majalis' I attended where the tragedy of Karbala would be relived in powerful prose, poetry and rhythmic chanting and beating of the chest.

But in Andhra Pradesh, Moharram had metamorphosed into something entirely different. In Hyderabad, it was mourning indeed for the Shia Muslims but when I travelled across the State during the Moharram season, I found this festival being 'celebrated' in every village and town in Telengana, Rayalaseema and parts of coastal Andhra Pradesh. Some tribal communities such as the Lambadies, Gonds and Pardies consider Moharram as important as Dussehra and Diwali. So popular is this festival that an entire body of Moharram folk songs in Telugu has evolved over the centuries. Solapur village in Rai Durg taluk of Rayalaseema was the home of well-known Telugu folk poet Ramana, who wrote a number of verses on Moharram.

An even better example of Hindu-Muslim syncretism is a Moharram song written by Balaiah, another Telugu folk poet:

> *Recite in the name of Allah,*
> *Then the Devata will bless you.*

How did a period of mourning get transformed into a joyous celebration? Moharram has its origins in the struggle for the Khilafat in the Muslim world that took place right after the Prophet's death. Shias reject many of the Khalifas as they consider the succession to the Prophet to be the special right of his family. The gulf between Shias and Sunnis was cemented after the battle of Karbala in AD 680, when the Khalifa's army fought and killed the Prophet's grandson Hazrat Hussain and seventy-two of his companions and family members, including many women and children. This tragedy is the central theme of the Shia faith and Moharram is this period of mourning.

Although Moharram continues for forty days, the first ten days are more important as the battle of Karbala was waged during these ten days. The tenth day is considered most significant as Imam Hussain died fighting that day. During this period, Shias wear black and organize several majalis, where a speaker always ends his address by giving an extremely evocative description of the events at Karbala. The majalis ends with mattam or beating of the chest. From the seventh to the tenth day of Moharram, numerous processions are taken out. These are among the oldest religious processions in the country. The main Bibi ka Alawa procession taken out by the Shias of Hyderabad on the tenth day of Moharram is, for instance, about four hundred years old. In contrast, Hindus began taking out processions on festivals like Ganesh Chaturthi and Durga Puja only about a hundred years ago.

The Bibi ka Alawa procession is a fearsome but riveting sight. It is led by an elephant carrying some sacred relics and includes many horses and camels. But the focus is on the groups of mourners who do mattam with chains, blades, knives and swords. Blood flows freely and is certainly not a sight for the squeamish. Mujtaba Ali Khan, a young college student who was doing mattam when we met him, explains the logic behind this self-flagellation and mutilation: 'It is our way of saying that if we had been at Karbala, Oh Hussain, we would have died fighting for you.'

A song of the Lambadi tribals describes an episode at Karbala when Imam Hussain saw his infant son die in front of his eyes while the rest of his family was denied water for many days:

Those arrows were not shot by brave men;
They were cowards.
The brave son of the brave father got injured;
He was the son of the bravest man,
In whose name we wear kantas.
It was not that he was not brave,
But he held his little son in his arms,
Who was shot dead.
He carried his son's dead body;
His family was thirsty;
He was surrounded by wolves,
Who kept shooting their arrows at him.

One institution that has played a key role in popularizing Moharram is the Ashurkhanas. These are buildings that house the Alams or copies of the staffs carried by Imam Hussain and his followers at Karbala. During Moharram, these Alams are taken out in several processions. Ever since the Qutb Shahi times, the doors of the Ashurkhanas have been thrown open and food and alms distributed to all, regardless of community or caste. Inside the Ashurkhanas, there are no restrictions and people are allowed to worship according to their own customs.

While a Muslim will only kiss the Alams and raise his hands towards God in prayer, one can see Hindus bow, fold their hands in prayer, garland the Alams, light incense sticks and do puja before them. Non-Muslims began to frequent the

Ashurkhanas not because they understood the tragedy of Karbala or suddenly began to believe in Islam but because they considered the Alams to be sacred objects that symbolised honesty, courage and piety. Superstition and wish-fulfilment played an important role in this process as people began to ask for mannat (boons) and some Ashurkhanas were credited with specific powers. At the Bibi ka Alawa Ashurkhana, for instance, from where the biggest Moharram procession of Hyderabad is taken out on the tenth day, large numbers of non-Muslim women pray to be blessed with children. In this manner, Hindu devotionalism is focused on Islamic motifs to create the uniquely Indian Moharram of the Deccan.

A folk song from Rangareddy district reveals how Moharram has been divested of its original identity and is considered a time of celebration when wishes are fulfilled and boons granted.

> Moharram brings joy and pleasure,
> All sorts of people happily meet at leisure,
> And make offerings in their devotion.
> The eager folks coming in groups,
> Enjoy themselves in the moonlit night,
> Those with stomach aches,
> Those with eye sores.
> Each and every one prays with devotion,
> And is relieved of the affliction;
> Hassan and Hussain and the happy Imam,
> Qasim dulah's palanquin has started, Twelve Imams.
> The vows taken have been fulfilled,
> And the boon of pregnancy granted to the sterile.

Aside from worshipping at the established Ashurkhanas, during Moharram, Hindu localities install their own Alams under makeshift tents. In Vijayanagram, I counted thirty roadside tents housing Alams. In most cases, a group of boys had set up a Moharram committee that collected funds from local residents and shopkeepers to hire tents, loudspeakers and the services of drumbeaters on the days that processions would be taken out. The atmosphere is exactly like that at a Hindu festival such as Ganesh Chaturthi: music blaring from loudspeakers installed above the Alams, offerings of coconuts and flowers, lighting of incense sticks, and processions led by drumbeaters.

That the local people considered the Alams no different from any of their deities was evident from the vermilion mark and garlands placed on the Alams. S. Balu, a tailor, who has been installing Alams in Vijayanagaram for several years, says: 'If you worship Pirulu (Alams), bad luck will stay away.' He knew nothing about Karbala and found it easier to equate Pirulu with Lord Rama. 'These (the Alams) are just called Pirulu. Just as we worship Rama, we pray to Pirulu.' The word Pirulu is obviously derived from Pir.

Back in Hyderabad, I found my room attendant at the government guest house on leave during the ninth and tenth day of Moharram. On being questioned, Jampaiah told me that he was a Lambadi tribal living in a basti in Banjara Hills and his community considered Moharram one of its biggest festivals. Every year they installed Alams in a jhuggi in the heart of their basti. And on the tenth night, the Alams would be taken out in a grand procession around the Banjara Hills.

Along the way, the Alams were immersed in a water tank for a few seconds, a completely non-Islamic ritual. Once the procession returns to the basti, merrymaking begins with both the men and women consuming country liquor and having a feast.

In the communally sensitive walled city, there are separate lanes called 'Hindu gullies' and 'Muslim gullies'. But the residents of old Hyderabad cannot completely isolate themselves from the influences of the other community. I attended a majalis in a Hindu lane called Sonar ki Gali. The host was Sudershan Das, a freedom fighter. He pointed out the three places where the Hindu residents of his lane had installed Alams. In Solapur village of Rayalaseema, I heard a group of Hindu farmers sing a beautiful Moharram song in Telugu.

The strange interpretation of Moharram makes us reflect on the following entry in the Hobson-Jobson dictionary:'...this example is followed by many of the Hindus... Moharram is celebrated throughout the Deccan and Malwa with greater enthusiasm than in other parts of India. Grand preparations are made in every town on the occasion, as if for a festival of rejoicing, rather than of observing the rites of mourning, as they ought.'

In Good Faith

MOUNTAIN COMES TO MOHAMMAD
Orissa

Strange things happen with religious practice in India. The Puri shrine is one of the premier temple complexes in the country that advocates its own brand of orthodoxy. The famed Rath Yatra of Lord Jagannath of Puri moves with great fanfare and amid great chaos. But one little detail that always goes unnoticed is that, at one point in its journey, the Jagannath rath halts in its tracks to pay respects to a Muslim saint-poet. This is a real 'Hindu' juggernaut and yet it stops briefly for a man of Muslim origin.

The story unfolded by both chance and design. When I travelled to Orissa to view what is billed as the greatest chariot festival in the world, I stopped over at Bhubaneswar en route to Puri. Across the road from the State guest house in Bhubaneswar is a tiny temple. On my way back from dinner, I chanced upon a small congregation of rickshaw pullers and daily wage earners singing Oriya bhajans at this roadside temple. As a friend translated the songs, I noticed that one of the singers in particular had an enchanting voice—he was Nakul Das, a construction worker. Das sang longingly of his desire to see Lord Jagannath:

> *O lord, I have waited the whole year long*
> *to behold you when you step out in your rath.*
> *Do not deny me this vision,*
> *cries your devotee, Salebeg.*

'Who is Salebeg?' I ask Das. Bhakta Salebeg, the great devotee who wrote most of the bhajans in Oriya praising Lord Jagannath, was a Muslim bhakta of the Lord. Every child in Orissa sings Salebeg's bhajans and knows his legend, was his reply. But how could a Musalman be a bhakta when the Puri temple does not admit non-Hindus? 'For Thakur (Lord Jagannath) was just a human being. Because he could not enter his temple, Thakur always stopped outside Salebeg's Puri home during the Rath Yatra. Even this year, Thakur's rath will halt outside Salebeg's samadhi.'

According to Professor A. K. Misra of Bhubaneswar University, who had done his doctorate on this special bhakta, Salebeg was the son of a Mughal nobleman, Jehangir Quli Khan Lalbeg, who was sent to Orissa around 1590 by Emperor Akbar, to assist Man Singh in quelling the Afghan rebels who still had considerable control over the eastern provinces. In Orissa, Lalbeg married a Brahmin widow who bore him a son, Salebeg, in 1592. When Jehangir succeeded Akbar to the Mughal throne at Agra, Lalbeg was made governor of the area which is now modern Bihar; two years later, he was made

governor of the Bengal province—which included Orissa—
and this is where the young Salebeg was raised.

Lalbeg eventually died on the battlefield fighting the Afghans.
Salebeg who fought alongside his father, was wounded. Legend
has it that his mother then asked him to pray to Lord Krishna.
He did so and, miraculously, his wounds healed. His father's
death proved to be a turning point in Salebeg's life and soon
after he became a devout Vaishnavite. As the leading Vaishnav
cult in Orissa was that of Lord Jagannath, Salebeg set up a
mutt in Puri near the Jagannath temple. He spent the rest of
life as a Bhakti saint and composed hundred of bhajans in
praise of Lord Jagannath. His hymns won him many admirers
and a cult soon gathered around the figure of Bhakta Salebeg.

There was, however, one major obstacle in Salebeg's path to
his Lord—the priests who controlled the Puri temple. For, no
matter how devout Salebeg may have been, in the eyes of the
pandas and pujaris, he was a mleccha (outcaste) and therefore
unfit to enter the Jagannath temple. In one bhajan Salebeg
bemoans his fate:

> *My father is a Musalman,*
> *My mother a Brahmin,*
> *But I, Salebeg, am only a poor devotee of my Lord Jagannath.*

To pay his respects to his Thakur, Salebeg would, therefore,
wait every year for the Rath Yatra, when Lord Jagannath left
his abode along with sister Subhadra and brother Balaram, to
visit his aunt who resided in the Gundicha temple. The week-
long Rath Yatra festival culminates with the return journey of
the three deities in their mighty chariots.

According to local tradition, one year Salebeg was returning from a pilgrimage to Vrindavan when the Rath Yatra began. While coming back to Puri, Salebeg prayed to Lord Jagannath not to deny him his annual darshan and help him reach in time for the return yatra. In fact, many of his bhajans deal with this desperate desire to reach Puri in time for the Rath Yatra. But when the return yatra began, Salebeg had still not reached Puri. The raths carrying Subhadra and Balaram always precede Lord Jagannath's chariot, and they went past Salebeg's mutt without awaiting his arrival. The legend goes that when Lord Jagannath's rath reached Salebeg's mutt, it came to a grinding halt. Hundreds of elephants and thousands of men could not make it budge. It was only after Salebeg arrived and pulled the ropes that Lord Jagannath resumed his yatra. Since then, the rath of Lord Jagannath always halts at Salebeg's samadhi during the return yatra.

The Rath Yatra is indeed a grand, much-publicized event. But this aspect of the festival has received little attention. In fact, the time I visited, Lord Jagannath's rath broke journey outside Salebeg's samadhi for the entire night! As the light faded and the crowds thinned, the mighty chariot carrying the Lord stopped in front of the modest samadhi of the Muslim devotee. In the dim light of hurricane lamps and the diyas offered by thousand of devotees, the huge rath cast its shadow over the tombstone.

The Hindu pantheon has numerous gods and goddesses jostling for supremacy. Orissa is perhaps the only part of the country where a single deity, Lord Jagannath, stands head and shoulders above the rest. Worshipped by both the high and low castes and even tribals, every home, shop and office in the State has an image of Lord Jagannath. Those huge, owl-shaped eyes of the Lord stare down from the backs of houses, walls and even posters and cinema hoardings. Lord Jagannath is omnipotent and omnipresent. It is, therefore, significant that a Muslim is irrevocably linked to his cult.

Salebeg's contribution to the Jagannath tradition can be gauged from the fact that the return of the rath to the Puri temple is heralded by a Salebeg samaroh every alternate year. This is the last night that Lord Jagannath spends in his rath just outside the temple gates before being taken inside early the next morning. The Salebeg samaroh, too, is held outside the temple gates where Orissa's leading vocalists render his compositions before an audience of thousands. Apart from their popularity, Salebeg's bhajans are considered among the finest devotional compositions of the Vaishnavite era. Besides the bhajans praising Lord Jagannath, he left behind a treasure trove of hymns and verses dedicated to Lord Krishna and other Vaishnav deities.

And just as a Muslim wrote the most popular bhajans for Lord Jagannath, one of the most accomplished Salebeg bhajan singers in the State also happens to be a Muslim—Sikander Alam. Like Salebeg, Sikander Alam, too, cannot enter the Puri temple. This is one of the great dualisms of the Hindu faith. On the one hand, it is inclusive and deity upon deity can be added to the pantheon. Yet there are centres of Hinduism that exclude and are certainly not egalitarian.

But an individual like Sikander Alam stands out in this age just as Salabeg did in another. The man has sung for more than forty Oriya films but is particularly famous for his renditions of the Jagannath bhajans. He is both a devout Muslim and a dedicated Jagannath bhakt. He says his namaz five times a day but his home in Bhubaneswar has several photographs of Hindu deities. His devotion is an example of the fact that nothing is absolute, and boundaries do not count for much.

LORD VISHNU'S LADY
Tiruchirapalli, Tamil Nadu

Lord Vishnu with a Muslim consort? The guardians of religious purity may squirm at the inter-religious coupling. But this, indeed, is a tradition preserved to date in the leading Vaishnav temple of Tamil Nadu—the Srirangam temple in Tiruchirapalli or Trichy.

In this huge temple complex (the largest in Tamil Nadu, perhaps even India), Lord Vishnu is known as Sri Ranganathaswamy and is depicted as reclining on the thousand-headed serpent of eternity. And one of his main consorts is Thulukka Nachiyar, which apparently means 'respected Muslim lady' in Tamil. The most important temple ceremony—famous across southern India—is the Vaikunta Ekadasi, which falls in the Tamil month of Margazhi (December-January) and lasts for twenty days. During the first ten days of the festival—called Pagal Pathu—Lord Vishnu is taken to Thulukka Nachiyar in a ceremonial procession. He is supposed to serve her for these ten days.

As Thulukka Nachiyar was a Muslim, no idol depicts her. There is, instead, a four-hundred-year-old Tanjore painting of a woman who represents her. Who was Thulukka Nachiyar? Legend has it that she was the daughter of a Muslim sultan who fell in love with Lord Vishnu. To please her, her father organized getting the statue stolen from temple. Devout worshippers, however, stole it back and retuned the stature to Srirangam. The sultan's daughter then came to the temple weeping for the darshan of her Lord. As she was not allowed in, she died weeping at the gates of the temple.

This legend was confirmed by the articulate P. Dhanapal, a deputy commissioner by rank who was the executive officer of the temple when I visited. He pointed out that there is little historical proof to back this legend about a sultan's daughter. All the same, the legend ends with Lord Vishnu accepting Thulukka Nachiyar as his consort. And the legend goes that as she died of a broken heart serving her Lord, it is now Lord Vishnu's turn to serve her during the Vaikunta Ekadasi festival.

As there is no historical evidence backing this legend, how then did the Brahmin guardians of Lord Vishnu admit a Muslim figure into the temple? No one has cared to study this tradition and provide a satisfactory explanation. Some academics in Tamil Nadu speculate that the tradition must have begun when the Arcot nawabs were the dominant power in the region during the eighteenth and nineteenth centuries. These Muslim rulers were never despoilers of temples; on the contrary, there is historical evidence that they made generous grants to many temples in the south, most notably the powerful Tirupati shrine, and the Srirangam temple. Trichy, in particular, was an important military base for the nawabs, and the town, therefore, received much of their largesse.

The guardians of powerful temples, such as the Srirangam and Tirupati shrines, must have found it necessary to strike some sort of compromise with the nawabs, who in time also became their benefactors. So just as the Muslim nawabs found it necessary to patronize the powerful temples of the region, the Brahmins, too, reciprocated by nominally incorporating Muslim figures into the various myths surrounding their major deity.

Dhanapal also agreed with this explanation. 'It is likely that this tradition was introduced at the time of Muslim rule,' he said, pointing out that many of the daily rituals at the temple also have shades of Muslim influence. For instance, there are six daily pujas before Lord Vishnu. During the first morning puja when the deity is bathed, he is made to wear a checked lungi, which is generally identified with Muslims in the region. Furthermore, during the second puja at 8.45 a.m., Lord Vishnu is made an offering of roti, dal and ghee—foods that he says are identified with Muslims in this rice-eating belt. But such generalizations are neither here nor there and cannot be taken too seriously.

What is undeniable is this curious Muslim consort. The Srirangam complex is not just another temple. It is a temple town of a fabulous gopuram and numerous shrines depicting the various avatars of Lord Vishnu with their consorts. It represents a tradition of unbroken religious activity for over a thousand years. It was from here that the Sri Ramanuja taught his concept of Bhakti yoga in the latter half of the eleventh century, which transformed Vaishnav philosophy throughout the country and produced numerous schools of thought.

It is a bustling hive of tourists and pilgrims. But while all are admitted into the complex, non-Hindus cannot enter the main gold-domed enclosure that the principal deity occupies. Ironically, it is inside this very enclosure that Thulukka Nachiyar, our 'respected Muslim lady', is housed as well. This particular Muslim has transcended boundaries between Islam and Hinduism, which other mortals are not allowed to cross.

GRAND TEMPLE, GRAND MOSQUE
Tiruchirapalli, Tamil Nadu

Trichy is not just an important Hindu pilgrimage centre (for, besides the Srirangam, the spectacular Rock Fort temples are also located here), it is also a major pilgrimage destination for Tamil Muslims. Not far from the Rock Fort complex is located the dargah of a Sufi saint called Nathar Vali, who many believe was among the first Muslim missionaries to settle in the Indian subcontinent. He is believed to have come to Trichy around the late tenth or early eleventh century, long before Moinuddin Chishti of Ajmer introduced Sufi philosophy in the north. Today, Nathar Vali's dargah is one of the biggest Sufi devotional centres in Tamil Nadu, attracting people of all faiths.

What is significant is that many links were established between the Hindu and Muslim religious centres of Trichy, particularly during the nineteenth and early twentieth centuries. For example, the two indentations atop the Rock Fort reflect an amalgamation of both religions, as one is considered the footprint of Nathar Vali, and the other that of Vishnu. According to Professor Hazrat Suhrahwardy, who is the younger brother of the saffadanashin (hereditary caretaker) of the Nathar Vali dargah, a scholar and an Urdu writer, 'Till recently Muslims used to attend a mela on the day after Eid on the site next to the Rock Fort temple which is associated with the saint Nathar Vali.'

The Cambridge historian, Susan Bayly, in her pioneering study of the minorities of South India titled *Saints, Goddesses and Kings: Muslims and Christians in South Indian Society 1700-1900*, writes: 'It has already been seen how closely the Srirangam shrine and the Nathar Vali dargah were related in the pre-colonial period. Their devotional traditions were full of shared motifs and legends, and their chronicles and shrine histories portrayed the two beings as counterparts of divine partners.' In fact, the Srirangam temple and the Nathar Vali dargah not only coordinate the celebrations of their festivals, but even share elephants and all other adornments.

Till the mid-1980s, both the Srirangam and the Rock Fort temples used to send their elephants to the dargah for the annual Moharram procession. Although that practice has now stopped, other local temples still loan their elephants for Moharram. More significant is the fact that the legends about the saint Nathar Vali are clearly derived from the local Hindu milieu. For one, the saint is often depicted in the coils of a giant cobra. This has nothing to do with Islam and is a part of folk tradition. The image is clearly inspired by the most powerful deity of the region—Lord Vishnu as Sri Ranganathaswamy, reclining on the giant serpent.

In Good Faith

There are other traditions at the dargah that, too, are inspired by Hindu customs. For instance, like their Hindu counterparts, the Muslims of this region also consider the waters of the river Cauvery to be sacred. During the Urs celebrations at the dargah, a procession goes to the river to collect holy water to wash the saint's grave with. This water is then distributed among devotees as tabarruk.

Bayly writes: 'Nathar Vali was one of the many Tamil power figures who transcended distinctions of Muslim and non-Muslim adherence. Even today, his cult attracts orthodox Chettir bazaar merchants as well as Hindu cultivators and artisans from localities all over southern and central Tamil Nadu.' This is indeed true and one sees many non-Muslim devotees at the dargah offering prayers in their own way by lighting oil lamps and seeking boons from the saint.

What is interesting to note is that many temple complexes of Tamil Nadu have received generous grants from the Arcot nawabs, the only Muslims to have ruled the region for a substantial period. Wealthy Muslim businessmen are still known to make grants to powerful temple complexes in the south. For instance, some years ago, a Muslim from Hyderabad presented a gold lotus worth lakhs of rupees to the Tirupati temple.

The nineteenth-century tradition of linkages between Hinduism and Islam may have weakened, but it still survives in parts of Tamil Nadu. This is largely because the Islam of Tamil Nadu is not an exclusive orthodox faith, but an entire body of beliefs and practices inspired as much by the local Hindu milieu as by Islamic tenets. This is an Islam which accommodates many of the pre-Islamic beliefs of the converts, where the Islamic ideal of egalitarianism combines with Vaishnav and Shaivite traditions to create a uniquely syncretic religion. Tamil Nadu is, in fact, the rare State where some Hindu temples and holy sites are also revered by Muslims. At Silamber near Chidambaram, for example, there is a temple to the popular Shaivite deity, Sri Murukan. Many Muslims revere this site as the throne of the prophet Sulaiman. Another popular cult surrounds the figure of Sikander, based on Alexander the Great, who is venerated as the precursor of a Muslim king. In Tamil Nadu, the Muslim hero Sikander is closely identified with the popular Hindu warrior deity called Subramanya or Skanda. The Sikander tradition is particularly strong in Madurai and there is a shrine atop a hillock on the outskirts of the city that is considered to be the abode of both Sikander and Subramanya/Skanda.

Again, the nature of popular Islam in this region has been tempered by the great devotional cults that sprang up around Sufi centres such as Nagore and Trichy. Even as they spread the message and attracted converts to the fold, the Sufi tombs also became one of the most powerful integrative bonds between Hindus and Muslims.

There is certainly a degree of give and take between the two communities. Take the two leading temples of Chennai: Kapaleeshwara and Parthasarathy. The temple tank of the Kapaleeshwara, an ancient Shiva temple in Chennai's Mylapore area, is used for the ceremonial immersion of the panjas or Alams carried by the Moharram procession. Till the nineteenth century, the tank of the Parthasarathy temple, located in the Muslim dominated Triplicane area of Chennai, was also used for the ceremonial immersion of Alams, in itself a syncretic custom.

The Parthasarathy temple was, in fact, richly endowed by the nawabs of Arcot, the only Muslims to have ruled part of Tamil Nadu. It is significant that the Arcot nawabs were never seen as despoilers of temples; on the contrary, they were considered benefactors of many major Hindu and Muslim shrines. Yet, as we have seen in earlier sections, localities with a history of symbiosis often have the first clashes. In 1990, Chennai recorded its first communal riot in recent history. The reason: the Vinayaka Chaturthi procession passing through the Muslim dominated Triplicane area raised provocative slogans and went on a rampage that resulted in three deaths. At that time, it was seen as the result of provocation by Hindutva forces who are today, perhaps, less relevant in the State.

ALL IN THE NADAR FAMILY
Tamil Nadu and Kerala

Both Christianity and Islam are perceived as being egalitarian religions, as against the caste-based hierarchy of Hinduism. But as the burning debate over the rights of Dalit Christians has revealed, the adoption of Christianity has not meant the end of the caste system. On the contrary, many Christian communities of South India continue to cling to their caste-based identities.

One such community is that of the Nadars. A Tamil-speaking people, Nadars are found throughout Tamil Nadu and at the tip of southern Kerala. In the social hierarchy of the south, Nadars would qualify as one of the more prosperous backward castes. Much of the Nadars' prosperity is, however, relatively recent. One of the more socially mobile communities of the south, they were originally known as 'Shanars' and their traditional occupation was toddy tapping and tenant farming. But as the Shanars made considerable economic and social gains through the late nineteenth and early twentieth centuries, they as a caste group adopted the new title of Nadar. Much of this advance was courtesy the Church; members of the community I spoke to say they have used Christianity as an instrument for social change although the original impetus to convert may have just been the desire to escape caste disadvantages.

But once the State granted certain basic rights to all lower castes, both Hindu and Christian, the conversions among the Nadars lost considerable momentum. Today, Nadars are both Christian and Hindu. While most Nadars in Tamil Nadu are Hindus, in some parts of Kanyakumari and Tirunelveli districts, Christian Nadars outnumber Hindus. In Kerala, about 70 per cent of the Nadars are Christians.

But what makes the Nadars a fascinating community is the fact that within the caste, religious differences often do not count. Marriages between Hindu and Christian Nadars are common and many Nadar families have members who practice both religions. Take the example of Sundaram Nadar, a wealthy trader in Kanyakumari. A devout Hindu, he makes it a point to go on the pilgrimage to Sabarimala in Kerala every year. His wife, however, belongs to the Protestant church.

At the other end of the socio-economic scale is Sreedharan Nadar, a bus conductor who lives in the Nadar dominated Neelimod village. Sreedharan is a Hindu, married to a Christian school teacher named D. Sumathi. There is no religious dispute in their home. Sumathi goes to church every Sunday while Sreedharan occasionally visits the local Bhadrakali temple.

What about the various religious ceremonies attached to marriage, childbirth or death, I asked Sreedharan? He replied,

'There is no complication. I will be cremated and my wife will be buried.' As for the marriage, Nadars follow a simple ceremony in the case of mixed marriages where the presence of a priest or pujari is not essential. The groom purifies a necklace known as thali, similar to a mangal sutra, in front of fire and ties it on the bride.

One result of such marriages is that Nadar names are often a mix of Hindu and Christian titles. Meet Leon Anthony Mohan, a motor vehicle inspector in the Kerala State government. He has a friend named Joseph Ram. And his brother Emmanuel Unni is married to a Hindu Nadar girl named Shailaja. Anthony told me: 'We have such wonderful names, either because of mixed marriages or because our families converted from Hinduism and also retained their Hindu names. My parents were Christian converts so they kept many Hindu customs. Mohan was my grandfather's name. Hence my name is Anthony Mohan.'

Charles, a former Congress MP from Thiruvananthapuram, is a Nadar. He had explained to me: 'For most Nadars, the caste affiliation is more important than [their] religious affiliation. That is why mixed marriages are common.' There is an irony in the fact that, though most Nadars who converted to Christianity did so to escape caste disadvantages, it is their caste that defines them. They have, however, in the course of time, overcome many social disadvantages.

Yet as with all communities, there is a greater focus on clear religious identities. Hence mixed marriages are on the decline. Indeed, some Nadars of Tamil Nadu support a fundamentalist organization like the Hindu Munnani that has carried out a strident campaign against conversion to both Christianity and Islam. Yet the community at large remains a fascinating study of social change and transformation of identity at multiple levels.

BEEMAPALLY'S LAMP
Kerala

Some years ago, there was a news report about a Kerala minister refusing to light an oil lamp at an inaugural function in Thiruvananthapuram on the grounds that it was an 'un-Islamic practice'. The minister was making it a point to stress the distinct and 'separate' identity of Kerala Muslims. The politician belonged to the Muslim League (IUML), whose position as the sole champion of the State's Muslims has been challenged by the recent rise of the Islamic Sevak Sangh (ISS), leading to a more-Islamic-than-thou posturing.

When I read this news report, my mind immediately went to the Beemapally shrine just outside Thiruvananthapuram and I contemplated the fact that the pious minister would consider many practices there quite reprehensible and certainly un-Islamic. He must also occasionally be troubled by the fact that many of the festivals celebrated by Kerala's Muslims are so clearly derived from the local Hindu environment. He could begin with a quick visit to the Beemapally shrine, which is dedicated to a Muslim lady, Beema Beevi, and is one of the most popular Muslim devotional centres in the State. The annual festival here, known as the Chandanakudam Mahotsavam, commemorates the death anniversary of Beema Beevi and is amongst the grandest Muslim celebrations in South Kerala that attracts tens of thousands of pilgrims from all communities. The rituals at the Chandanakudam are derived from local folk customs and have no Islamic roots whatsoever. The festival gets its name from small earthen pots called chandanakudam that are offered by pilgrims. Burning incense sticks are thrust into the opening of the chandanakudams that the devotees carry on their heads. One can only presume that a mindset that considers lighting an oil lamp as un-Islamic would certainly not approve of incense sticks.

Amongst the other rituals seen at the Beemapally festival are the dahara muttu, a kind of game which includes singing, beating small drums and moving the body in a particular rhythm; ratheeb, which involves acts of self-immolation; and kolkali or 'stick play' when two or more men dance and display various feats with wooden sticks. All these rituals are inspired by Hindu customs. For instance, ratheeb is derived from a custom followed in Kerala's Hindu temples known as kumaram when a folk priest cuts his forehead with a knife, gets into a trance and starts chanting like an oracle. And kolkali can trace its origins to the traditional fencing schools called kalaris where upper-caste Nayars were trained in warfare.

The Beemapally festival ends on the tenth day when the traditional flag of the dargah is taken out in a grand procession known as Pattanapravesam that traverses about one kilometre around the shrine. The president of the dargah's managing committee mounts a caparisoned elephant holding the flag in his hand. Two more elephants lead the procession while troupes of dancers and performers follow. Once the procession returns to the shrine, a grand fireworks display begins and continues till daybreak. The use of elephants and fireworks at Muslim festivals has undoubtedly been borrowed directly from temple celebrations in the State—such as the Trichur temple festival—that are known for extravagant elephant parades and lavish displays of fireworks.

The Beemapally Chandanakudam is part of the tradition of saint-martyr worship popular in Kerala known as nerccas. The largest public festivals of Kerala's Muslim community are the nerccas that combine nominally Islamic motifs with indigenous folk festivals. After visiting Beemapally, I had called on historian M. Gangadhara Menon at his home near Kozhikode. Along with Stephen Dale, he had written a significant paper titled *Nerccas: Saint-Martyr Worship among the Muslims of Kerala*. In the paper, they write: 'All the festivals are conducted within a ritual framework derived from the worship of folk deities in Kerala. The nerccas are important because of this hybrid character.' They conclude that these non-Muslim festivals have taken on a uniquely Muslim flavour for two reasons. 'First, nerccas, like velas and purams, are seasonal: all three appear to have originated as harvest festivals. Second, nerccas share a common ceremonial pattern with most velas and purams.'

The basic rituals of the nerccas are organized by the tannals, leaders of the Kerala Muslim clergy. The most important

The Bauls of Bengal wander from village to town, strumming their ektaras and singing of a universal God.

Makeshift temples of the Muslim goddess, Bonbibi, line the Sundarban forests.

Alams being worshipped in Hyderabad.

The Nagore dargah in Tamil Nadu is one of the main Sufi centres in the State.

*The Kanifnath Kanobha shrine in
Ahmadnagar was originally a mazhaar.*

*The Rath Yatra of Lord Jagannath at Puri moves amidst
much fanfare and chaos.*

Deva Sharif, the impressive mausoleum of Waris Shah.

The Patachitra painters of Bengal live on the periphery of two religions and have adapted the best of both Hinduism and Islam.

The Srirangam Temple in Tiruchirapalli houses Lord Vishnu and his Muslim consort, Thulukka Nachiyar.

The Ramdeora shrine in Jaisalmer district is the main pilgrimage centre of the Ramdeo Baba cult, which is particularly popular with Dalits and lower castes.

The Vailankanni Church in Tamil Nadu attracts about two million pilgrims every year.

The Manganiyar musicians of Rajasthan profess Islam but have a lifestyle remarkably similar to that of Hindus.

offering at each nercca is presented in a highly stylized ritual by groups representing entire villages, castes or occupational associations. Each group pays its respects to the tannals before proceeding to the shrine where the offering is made before a metal lamp known as nilavilakku, which is found in the homes of most Kerala Hindus. The Imam of the Palayam Masjid in Thiruvananthapuram, who publicly lauded the minister's refusal to light an oil lamp, should perhaps ponder if this practice, too, is 'un-Islamic'.

The nerccas are an important source for studying the history and culture of the Muslim community in Kerala. Every aspect of Muslim life in the State has been influenced in varying degrees by the local non-Muslim environment. The history of Islam in Kerala is as old as Islam itself, as Arab traders are believed to have sailed between Kerala and Arabia during the lifetime of the Prophet himself. By the ninth century, Arabs had small pockets in many Malabar towns. The numbers of Muslims multiplied as the Arabs married local women and produced a community known as Mappila, which means son-in-law, an indicator of the excellent relations between the early Muslim traders and the local population.

By the twelfth century, there were several mosques in Kerala. The Cheraman Perumal Juma Masjid in Kodungallur was the first mosque in the subcontinent, which some maintain was built in the lifetime of the Prophet. This mosque is believed to have been designed and constructed by Hindus as its architecture was similar to the design of temples in Kerala. But during a visit to Kodungallur, I was stunned to discover that the old peaked and tiled building had been pulled down by the community itself in 1985 and replaced by a garish, modern structure. All the mosques of the Mappilas built before this century followed the architectural model of local Hindu temples, reflecting not only the Mappilas' integrating in Kerala's culture, but also their isolation from North Indian Islam.

The Mappilas borrowed many social customs from Hinduism as well. For example, their marriage ceremonies involve tying the thali and exchanging garlands, like in any Hindu wedding. Some Muslims of Kozhikode and Kannur even adopted the local Nayar customs of matriliny, joint family and visiting husbands, which survive to date among many families though it has no precedent in Islam. Even the Ali Rajas who founded the first Mappila kingdom in the fourteenth century followed matriliny. They were arguably the only Muslim dynasty in the world with a matrilineal order of inheritance. Several heads of the family have been women bearing the title 'Bibi' and even today, there is a Bibi of Kannur.

There has been constant give and take between the Mappilas and the Hindus of Kerala. Many Muslims have made rich contributions to the development of the Malayalam language and literature. The greatest living Malayalam writer is Vaikom Muhammad Basheer; while one the biggest film stars, Mammootty—whose name is derived from Muhammad Kutty—is also a Muslim. In spite of a great integration and the commonality of language and culture, Kerala's Muslims increasingly stress their distinctiveness in political choices that some may see as conservative.

THE MUSIC BRIDGE
Jodhpur, Rajasthan

Folk music is an intrinsic part of the sights and sounds of Rajasthan. Any visitor to the State would have come across tiny groups of musicians with their colourful turbans and string instruments. This is not just a spectacle put up for tourists but an integral part of the desert culture. There are entire hereditary castes of musicians, among whom the Langas and Manganiyars are the most accomplished. What makes these musician castes unique is that many of them, such as the Langas and the Manganiyars, while professing Islam through their customs and dress, have a lifestyle remarkably similar to that of Hindus.

I was fortunate to have met and extensively interview the late Komal Kothari for this book. The legendary folklorist and musicologist spent a lifetime documenting Rajasthan folklore, arts and crafts. Indeed, he is the one individual who possibly made the largest contribution to the understanding and promotion of the musician communities of Rajasthan. In a monograph on the Langas, he has written about how the conversion of the Langas created a diffused culture where many Hindu customs were retained. The dress was also retained. For instance, men continued wearing dhotis and women the heavy bangles known as chuda that signify marriage. Ceremonies attached to lifecycles such as marriage and birth were retained.

I had several meetings with Kothari at his Jodhpur house, and at every meeting, he would come up with fascinating statistics. According to him, about 80 per cent of the folk musicians of Rajasthan are Muslims though their patrons are mostly Hindus. Particularly in the desert districts of Jaisalmer, Banner, Bikaner and Jodhpur, it is Muslim musicians who perform at various ceremonies such as marriages, births and even festivals at Hindu homes.

The Manganiyars, for instance, have a number of songs on Hindu festivals and sing bhajans composed by the Bhakti saints. The main patrons of the Langas, however, have traditionally been the Sindhi Sipahis. The Sindhi Sipahis are a small Muslim community made up primarily of cattle-keepers or herdsmen. In the traditional system of patronage, each Langa family has the right to sing or perform at certain homes of the Sindhi Sipahis. This system does not imply that the patrons are more prosperous than the musicians. The Langas and the Sindhi Sipahis belong to the same economic strata and are representative of the fact that Rajasthani folk culture continues to be supported by the rural masses, and not the rare feudal overlord.

Today, however, a new system of patronage has evolved with the popularization of the music of the Langas and the

Manganiyars. This patronage is not based on the hereditary right to perform but on the excellence of the musicians. Now, the more accomplished singers and sarangi players among the Langas regularly travel outside the country for the various international festivals showcasing India, as well as travel from city to city within the country popularizing the vibrant folk music of the desert. This has been followed up by recording contracts, with established companies bringing out high quality recordings of the music of the Langas and Manganiyars.

The Langas are a small community—less than three thousand today. They play two types of sarangies known as the Sindhi Sarangi or the Gujaratan Sarangi. Neither of these instruments is easily available. They preserve their art by handing down their precious sarangies from generation to generation, just as their songs are handed down from father to son. Women do not sing or perform.

The popularization of the Langas' music has played an important role in preserving this art. Though the people of Rajasthan have been able to sustain the Langas till today, their dwindling numbers indicate that it is unlikely their way of life would have survived without the sudden prosperity that came their way. There is now a settlement of the community in a small Jodhpur town known as Langa Colony, whose residents make a living through recordings and live performances. I remember Kothari telling me that when he first asked the Langas to sing before a microphone, they feared that this gadget would steal their music. Today, many are sophisticated performers, wearied by the concert circuit.

With their music and way of life, they are an enduring symbol of life in the desert and the richness of a joint heritage.

WHERE A CULT CONQUERS CASTE
Pokhran, Rajasthan

Rajasthan is one of those parts of the country where folk deities have a far greater following than the Brahmanical high gods. The five major folk gods of the State are Tejaji, Pabuji, Mehaji, Gogaji and Ramdeoji, and of these five, the last two—Gogaji and Ramdeo Baba—are worshipped by Muslims as well, making Rajasthani folk religion an example of a synthesis of what we define as Hindu and Muslim.

The Ramdeo Baba cult, in particular, is a fascinating amalgam of popular lore. Ramdeo Baba is the deity of all the lower castes, both Hindu and Muslim. While Hindus consider him to be an avatar of Vishnu, Muslims believe that Baba Ramdeo is the reincarnation of a Sufi saint named Samas Pir, and refer to him as Ramsa Pir. There is even a small section of Sikhs who worship the Baba as the reincarnation of the tenth guru. Ramdeo Baba is, therefore, one of those rare deities venerated by members of three religions—Hindus, Muslims and Sikhs.

And this is no obscure cult, but one of the most popular religious traditions of Rajasthan. Shrines to Ramdeo Baba are found in hundreds of villages across the State. The main temple is located in the Ramdevra village of Jaisalmer district, about 13 kilometres from Pokhran. Thousands crowd this tiny village during the annual fair held between Bhadon Sudi 2 and Bhadon Sudi 11. The famous Rajasthani dance known as Terah Taal is performed here during the festival.

Ramdeo Baba is believed to have been a Tomar Rajput who dedicated his life to fighting the caste system and uplifting the poor. Today, he is perceived as an invincible hero who comes to the aid of the needy in times of drought and crisis, and is depicted as a rider on a white horse. His closest disciple was an untouchable girl named Dali Bai whose samadhi is opposite the structure housing Ramdeo Baba's memorial. This cult is, therefore, particularly popular with the lower castes and Dalits. In the village shrines dedicated to Ramdeo Baba, even the officiating priests are from the lower castes. At the main Ramdeora shrine, however, the Baba's Tomar Rajput descendants are in control and serve as priests.

When I visited Ramdeora on a hot April day, I struck up a conversation with a local guide who then took me to the shrine. The guide, Beldar, was a Dalit and it soon became evident that there was hostility between the Rajput caretakers of the shrine and members of the lower castes, who have traditionally made their livelihood from serving pilgrims. According to Beldar and a Harijan sweeper, Badami, who worked at the shrine, the Rajputs were slowly depriving the lower castes of their rightful share of the income from the temple. The tussle was over the lakhs of rupees earned by the shrine and while the bulk of the money has always gone to the Tomar Rajputs, the lower castes have traditionally had a share of the offering. Over the years, however, the lower castes say they have been marginalized, with the Rajputs appropriating all the profits for themselves.

Another interesting discovery at the shrine was the attempt to minimise the importance of the Muslim connection to the cult and connect Baba Ramdeo to the Brahmanical gods of the Hindu pantheon. I was told by a regular Rajput devotee: 'He is an avatar of Lord Rama and like Lord Rama, he had gone on a vanvas for fourteen years. All this about him being a Pir is spread by illiterate people who know nothing of Hinduism.'

Such attempts by a handful of Hindu purists cannot, however, change the fact that the legend of Baba Ramdeo depicts him as a folk hero who was the avatar of a Pir. The entry on Ramdeora village in the *Jaisalmer District Gazetteer* notes: 'There exists no written record about the origin of the village but there is a legend which says that Ramdeoji took samadhi here in 1458... Ramdeoji is worshipped by Hindus and Muslims alike... He became renowned as a saint in Marwar and his fame spread far and wide. It is said that five Pirs from Mecca arrived to test his powers. They were offered food and milk by Ramdeoji who, seeing that they were without utensils, brought their pots from Mecca by his supernatural powers. Convinced of his powers, the Pirs paid their homage to Ramdeoji. Ever since, he has been worshipped as Ramsa Pir by the Muslims.'

The more elaborate version of this legend was recounted to me by the late folklorist Komal Kothari. According to this version, a childless Hindu king went to a number of Hindu saints who were unable to grant him a son. These holy men, however, told the king about a great Pir in Benaras (now Varanasi) called Samas Pir who could perform miracles. The Rajput king went to Samas Pir and asked him for a son and added that he would be even more blessed if the Pir himself could be reborn as his son. This is how Samas Pir came to be reborn as Ramdeoji in a Tomar Rajput home. The five Pirs came to see whether Ramdeoji really was Samas Pir and were convinced after his display of miraculous powers. They then bowed in reverence before Ramdeoji.

A week later, I heard an even more elaborate and colourful version of this legend from a Muslim musician in the desert village of Kanhoi, not far from the famous sand dunes of Jaisalmer. There, Murad Manganiyar regaled us with a long and winding tale about Samas Pir and Baba Ramdeo. Incidentally, the name Ramsa Pir, as the Muslims call Ramdeoji, is derived from combining Ram with Samas.

Later, when I told Kothari about our experiences at the shrine, he agreed that 'there is an attempt to "Sankritize" the cult and the Pir element has been getting less importance over the years'. All the same, he believed 'that it will be impossible to transform this most humane of religious cults into an orthodox Hindu tradition'. After all, if Ramdeo Baba is revered across the State, it is because he stood against caste and religious divisions. This tradition is kept alive, not by the higher castes, but by people from the lower levels of society who have nothing to gain by erecting barriers of caste and religion.

MUSLIM DESCENDANTS OF ARJUNA
Alwar, Rajasthan

Like other capital cities of the world, Delhi is a city obsessed with itself. The capital's influential and always-expanding tribe of intellectuals often pontificate on and plan the state of the nation without stepping outside the city limits. And in the last decade, perhaps no subject has received as much attention as the Muslim community. Reams have been written on the Muslim 'psyche'; on the community's response to the emergence of the Hindu Right; on the orthodoxy's hold on the community; on terrorists being bred and the flip side of the 'fear psychosis' gripping it. And come election time, every publication devotes precious newsprint to speculating on that mythical thing called the 'Muslim vote'. Every reputable columnist in the city has, at some time or the other, expressed an opinion on the Muslim community.

But all these opinion-makers—whether belonging to the liberal Left or the Right—tend to describe the Muslim society in absolute terms. Hindu society is plural but Muslims are believed to constitute a huge monolithic mass. The facts belie this view. The only thing uniform about the Muslims of India is their diverse cultural zones. Even the brand of Islam followed by Indian Muslims varies from region to region. Few seem to be aware that there are numerous Muslim communities who profess Islam but remain steeped in the local Hindu ethos.

For instance, just outside the city boundaries begins the large pocket where the Meo Muslims live. These Muslims profess Islam but follow a fascinating composite culture that accommodates many Hindu customs. They trace their origins to Hindu figures such as Rama, Krishna and Arjuna and celebrate many Hindu festivals like Diwali, Dussehra and Holi.

And the Meos are no obscure tiny sect; they are a 400,000-strong community found in the region known as Mewat, which is spread across the border areas of the three states of Uttar Pradesh, Haryana and Rajasthan. In Uttar Pradesh, they are found in the Chhata tehsil while in Haryana, the Meos occupy the Nuh and Ferozepur tehsils of Gurgaon district. But the area where the Meos dominate and have been able to preserve their unique culture is the Alwar district of Rajasthan, just a two-hour drive from Delhi.

The Meos are famous across the Mewat belt for their narration of folk epics and ballads. Their oral tradition is a rich source for studying and understanding the community's history. Among the epics and ballads sung by the Meos, which are derived from Hindu lore, the most popular is the Pandun ka kada, the Mewati version of the Mahabharata. Many Meos also trace their origins through the epic which describes them as descendants of Arjuna.

The Meos have a distinct identity, separating them from both mainstream Hindu and Muslim society. Their marriages combine the Islamic nikaah ceremony with a number of Hindu rituals— like maintaining exhaustive gotras, a distinctly Hindu practice. One fascinating tradition still preserved by Meos is the tracing of their genealogy by Hindu genealogists known as jaggas. The jaggas are an essential part of any lifecycle ceremony in the Meo community.

The Meos are believed to have gradually converted to Islam between the twelfth and the sixteenth centuries. Their Hindu origins are evident from their names, as most Meos still keep the title 'Singh', revealing the syncretic nature of the community. Ram Singh, Til Singh and Fateh Singh are typical Meo names. I met Fateh Singh, a Meo balladeer in a village on the outskirts of Alwar. After reciting the Pandun ka kada, he spoke at length on what he believed to be the community's origins.

Fateh Singh and his fellow villagers firmly believe that they are Kshatriyas descending from Arjuna who gradually converted to Islam under the influence of Sufi Pirs. But they told me that the Meos are gradually giving up the celebration of Hindu festivals. 'If you go into villages in the interior, you will see that the Meos are just like Hindus. You will not be able to make out the difference between Meos and Hindu villagers. But near the city, more and more people are giving up Hindu customs and rituals.'

It is not difficult to trace the reason for this. The Ayodhya agitation and its aftermath succeeded in infusing the communal virus even into the peaceful Mewat belt. The Babri demolition had resulted in violence in the region. Ever since, political alignments and mobilization has been on community lines. In 2011-12, there was vicious communal violence in Mewat and the Muslim community there accuses the State government of targeting them in a shooting that left over ten dead in a village.

The identity question in the Mewat belt, therefore, is being raised in a complex and changing landscape. Moreover, as one Meo villager told me when I travelled there in 2011: 'Ever since the RSS and the BJP became a powerful political force in the State, more and more Meos have begun to identify themselves as Muslims.' The orthodoxy naturally has an opportunity to show the faithful the correct path according to them. There is, therefore, a far greater self-consciousness about being a Muslim. As Chandan Singh, a schoolteacher put it: 'Increasingly, the mullahs tell Meos that they are bad Muslims and that they must give up celebrating Hindu festivals if they want to be accepted by the Muslim society.' According to him, one can see evidence of the slow Islamization of the Meos in the number of mosques that have sprung up over the last decade. 'Earlier, most Meos never went to the masjid. Now, so much money has come in for the construction of masjids from religious institutions funded by Gulf money, that the Meos are increasingly turning to the Islamic way of life.'

Earlier, all Meos traced their origins to Arjuna through the Pandun ka kada. But as a result of this deliberate Islamization, epics such as the *Shamsher Pathan* and *Behram Badshah*—which suggest that the Meos came from Arabia—are also gaining in popularity. Caught between the pincer of Hindu fundamentalism on one side and Islamic puritanism on the other, most syncretic communities in India are undergoing a gradual transformation and the Meos are no exception. But what is remarkable is that they have still retained much of their old ways of life. One does not have to search too hard to find a Meo singing the Pandun ka kada or celebrating Dussehra. They still remain a fascinating testament to a shared history, a shared culture in the subcontinent.

SATI DEVI'S MUSLIM BALLADEERS
Jaisalmer, Rajasthan

F ew parts of the country have as rich a folk tradition as
Rajasthan; be it in its music or its folk myths, Rajasthan
never ceases to amaze. The State simply abounds in the
improbable and incredible. For instance, one of the most
popular sati cults in the State is preserved and propagated by
Muslim musicians! More amazing is the fact that this particular
sati immolated herself, not on her husband's funeral pyre, but
on that of her devar's (younger brother-in-law), who is believed
to have been her lover. For this act of passion, she was promptly
deified and is today worshipped as a Devi throughout the
desert district of Jaisalmer.

Known as the Bhattiani Sati Rani, her legend goes something
like this: a Rajput belonging to the Bhatti clan of Jaisalmer, she
was married off to a powerful Rathore Rajput from Jalor in
Barmer district. The more straitlaced version of her legend
has it that she committed sati on her brother-in-law's pyre, not

because the two were lovers, but because she was misinformed that her husband had perished in battle whereas it was really the devar who had died. The more popular version is spicier: that our lady had taken her devar as her lover and, unable to bear the grief of losing him, committed her scandalous sati on his funeral pyre.

The transformation from notoriety to divinity is even more fantastic. Apparently, after the act of immolation, the in-laws did not even care to complete the last rites of the Bhattiani Rani. Her family fled when her spirit began to haunt their house, wreaking vengeance on any unfortunate soul who crossed her path. She had by now taken on the form of a blood-thirsty Kali-like Devi who sought appeasement.

It is at this point in the legend that Muslim folk singers are linked to the Bhattiani Sati cult. One day, a Muslim musician is believed to have come across the fearsome Sati Devi. To save himself from the Devi's wrath, he promised to build her a shrine and to immortalize her legend through his songs. From then on, the Muslim folk singers of Jaisalmer district known as the Manganiyars have been singing hymns of praise to this sati.

The Manganiyars' association with this sati cult can also be explained by the fact that they are a very syncretic Muslim community. Over 80 per cent of the folk musicians of the desert belt are Muslim; of these the hereditary caste of Manganiyars are amongst the most accomplished. As all their patrons are Hindu villagers, most of the Manganiyars' songs are about Hindu marriages, births and festivals and even include bhajans. Hence it would not be considered extraordinary for the Manganiyars to include songs about a Sati Devi in their repertoire.

Because the Manganiyars are inextricably linked to the origins of the Bhattiani Sati cult, they have the right to sing and collect a part of the offerings at every shrine dedicated to her. And though Rajasthan abounds in sati shrines, few have acquired the sort of cult following achieved by the Bhattiani Rani. Hers is among the most important sati cults of Rajasthan, particularly in Jaisalmer district. Tiny shrines dedicated to the Bhattiani Sati Rani are found in any number of villages here.

The two largest shrines to the Bhattiani Sati are, however, in her husband's hometown, Jalor, in Barmer district, and in Jaisalmer town. In the heart of Jaisalmer, not far from the railway station, stands one of the main Bhattiani Sati temples. A medium-sized structure surrounded by a courtyard, it is, however, the site for two of the largest religious melas in the town. Twice a year, thousands crowd the temple for a darshan of Sati Devi.

That is the best season for the Manganiyars who regularly sing at the temple. When we visited the temple on a sleepy April afternoon, there were three Manganiyars present— Kamruddin, Fakirchand and Firoz Gul. All of them were accomplished musicians who claimed that they sang at the temple, not for monetary gain, but because of a firm belief in Sati Devi. Kamruddin, in fact, turned out to be a minor celebrity; a regular performer on All India Radio, he claimed to have sung some folk songs for the award-winning film, *Rudaali*. As proof, he proudly displayed photographs of himself with the cast—Dimple Kapadia et al.

Fakirchand was an entirely different proposition. In ominous tones, he warned us that we might get struck down by some mysterious disease if we did not pay proper obeisance to Sati Devi. Just in case we missed the point, he introduced us to Gopi Bai, a sort of resident oracle who would regularly get into trances when she claimed to be speaking on behalf of Sati Devi. We beat a hasty retreat just when Gopi Bai threatened to swoon and let out fearful utterances against shameless non-believers like us.

At the gate we were accosted by Bal Dev Vyas, the caretaker of the shrine, who proudly informed us that he did not allow scheduled caste devotees to enter the main temple. 'They can pray from outside,' he added generously. Vyas had obviously not heard about Dalit empowerment.

On that note, we left this strange little sati mandir which permitted Muslims into the sanctum sanctorum but did not allow low-caste Hindus to set foot inside the structure.

A MECCA IN A MANDIR
Ayodhya, Uttar Pradesh

(This article was written four days after the Babri Masjid had been demolished by a mob in Ayodhya. Many of us believed that day marked the beginning of the unravelling of the Indian secular project. I was in Delhi when the mosque disappeared in a haze of dust and watched it on the BBC. I wept, as did many friends and family. The next day, I travelled to Lucknow to visit my family, then to Faizabad and Ayodhya.)

It has been four days since the Babri Masjid was demolished. I am staying with a wealthy Muslim family in Faizabad, the district headquarters and the twin city attached to Ayodhya. The house is bang opposite the residence of the district collector, but our host lives in the mortal fear that he and his family will be attacked. He has removed his nameplate and told members of his family to stop looking 'like Muslims'. He has not been to Ayodhya, just a few kilometres away, since the Ram Janmabhoomi agitation began. I ask him to accompany me to Ayodhya now that the Babri Masjid has been reduced to rubble and the mob has gone. He argues that it is still unsafe for a Muslim to go to Ayodhya. 'How will anyone know that you are a Muslim?' I ask. He replies, 'They know. They always know.'

During an earlier trip, a month before the demolition, I had come across a curious cast of characters in Ayodhya. In spite of a large police presence, the town was clearly in the hands of Hindu extremists who believed that the medieval mosque stood on the debris of a Hindu temple that marked the birthplace of Lord Rama. The air was thick with anticipation and there was a childish excitement amongst the ranks of the Rama devotees. The younger volunteers laughed quickly and animatedly; their eyes glazed with the sheer machismo of the act they hoped to perform. For all the protestations later made by BJP leaders, it was clear that the foot soldiers had made their own plans. Any visitor to Ayodhya in November 2002 would have sensed that an apocalyptic event was round the corner.

That month, when the Babri mosque still dominated the Ayodhya skyline, I met Ansar Hussain, then eighty-seven years old, but still mentally alert. For the last forty-five years, Hussain, better known as Munnu Baba, had been the caretaker-manager of Sunder Bhawan, one of the many Rama temples in Ayodhya, just a kilometre from the mosque site. It was a curious arrangement for a practising Muslim to be appointed caretaker of a temple in a Hindu pilgrimage town. It was the eccentricity of a minor feudatory from the neighbouring Bastar district that led to this arrangement. Though the Sunder Bhawan was built in 1947, the year of the Partition, its Hindu owners did not hesitate to hand over charge of the temple to a Muslim. Since then, Hussain had kept his side of the bargain. Having survived the upheaval of the Partition, he did not believe that his life or livelihood faced any threat in Ayodhya that winter. Hindus, he said, are a very peace-loving people. 'These are bogus threats. All politics. No one will touch the Babri mosque.'

When I returned to Ayodhya four days after the demolition, there was no sign of Hussain. There was a big lock on his door. His Muslim neighbours, too, had vanished. At the temple he cared for so many years, a young boy with a saffron scarf said he had no idea where Hussain had gone, but it would be good for everyone if he had left Ayodhya as he was polluting the gods. 'He was a stubborn old fool.'

Hussain had told me that two years ago, when he had fallen seriously ill and needed a blood transfusion, two sadhus of the Hanuman Garhi temple, the premier mandir in Ayodhya, had donated their blood. Did the infamous 6 December mob, baying for the blood of Muslims, spare Hussain? Did the sadhus who had once donated their blood also get swept off by the heat of the moment, and now wished to draw blood?

Almost as if to make up for not finding Hussain, I came across another stubborn old fool that afternoon. This one lived less than half a kilometre away from the Babri site. His name was Laljibhai Satyasneha, a Gandhian and follower of a Swami who went by the name of Satyabhakt (true devotee). Laljibhai had set up a somewhat bizarre temple in the midst of a town that was devoted almost exclusively to worshipping the warrior-king Lord Rama and Hanuman. In Laljibhai's Satyar Mandir, idols of Rama and Krishna stood alongside Christ, Buddha and Mahavira, the founder of the Jain faith. The idols were flanked on both sides by pictures of Mecca and Medina. Laljibhai was scathing in his indictment of the new age Rama devotees. 'They are not practicing Hinduism. History will not forgive them for taking a non-violent faith and making it ugly and destructive.'

But he made another point that was worth exploring. Laljibhai believed that in their quest for political power, the votaries of the new aggressive Hinduism, had, ironically, borrowed liberally from the very group they abhorred—Muslims. On reflection, it was easy to see the Hindutva brigade's attempt to 'semitise' Hinduism. Consider the following examples: all Rama cadres were told to turn in the direction of Ayodhya and pray on a particular day, similar to Muslims offering prayers in the direction of Mecca. The Rama devotees marched in processions and expressed a willingness to die for the temple; martyrdom is a hallowed concept in Islam but not in Hinduism. They brandished swords and some had carved Jai Sri Ram on their chests; an image not very different from the Moharram processions of Shia Muslims. And finally, swarms of sadhus and holy men belonging to different sects were suddenly united in their quest for a temple; was it an attempt to create a Hindu clergy that could yield the kind of authority that the mullahs claim to have over the Muslim community?

That is why Laljibhai insisted that the new age Hindus had to be fought, not to save Indian Muslims, but to rescue

Hinduism from its hijackers. That season in Ayodhya, Laljibhai, frequently threatened and heckled by his co-religionists, came across as a quaint, tragic-comic figure. He said nice things about secularism but was sadly out of touch with the times. Who would heed his calm words when the feverish shrieks for the destruction of a mosque proved so much headier? The cacophony of the mob drowned his voice of dissent that winter.

(I returned to Ayodhya in January 2012 and discovered that the Satyar Mandir still survives in a building known as the Gujarat Bhawan, although Laljibhai passed away three years ago. Old-timers in the temple town tell me that he came from Wardha in Gujarat and there is a similar temple there with an additional picture—that of Karl Marx.

I also learnt that some months after the demolition of the Babri Masjid, Ansar Hussain and his family returned to Ayodhya. He resumed looking after the Sita-Rama mandir until he, too, passed away some years ago.)

THE SUFI OF SALON
Rae Bareli, Uttar Pradesh

The matrix of language, culture, music, politics of identity and symbology is perhaps most complex in Uttar Pradesh. The State was the cradle of the Ram Janmabhoomi movement and some of the worst communal riots in independent India have taken place here—in Meerut, Moradabad, Kanpur, Varanasi, Aligarh, Gonda...

On the other hand, this region has also known some of the closest Hindu-Muslim interaction in the country. This synthesis has influenced every aspect of life and culture of the region—language, literature, music and architecture as is seen in the mingling of Hindu and Islamic architectural styles at the Fatehpur Sikri and in the syncretic origins of the Urdu language itself.

It is perhaps in the fields of language and music that Muslims have made the maximum contribution. Some of the greatest poets, writers and figures in the history of North Indian classical music have been Muslims. What is less celebrated is the contribution of Muslims to the development of folk music and regional dialects like Braj Bhasha and Awadhi. The vast majority of the rural folk of eastern UP, for instance, speak neither Urdu nor Hindi, but Awadhi. And some of the most popular Awadhi songs of the Rae Bareli district—sung in both Hindu and Muslim homes—have been composed by a Sufi saint known as Shah Naim Ata.

Ata came from an illustrious line of Sufis belonging to the Chishtiya order settled in Salon, a tiny township in the Rae Bareli district. The founder of the khanqah was one Sheikh Pir Mohammad who set up his abode in Salon with a Hindu sanyasi in the seventeenth century. After his death in 1687, his son Mohammad Ashraf became the first Sajjada Nashin (hereditary caretaker) of the dargah. But the best-known figure attached to this dargah was the eighth Sajjada Nashin, Shah Mohammad Naim Ata, who passed away in 1966 after being head of the dargah for sixty-six years.

Shah Naim Ata's contribution to the local dialect and musical traditions of the region is incalculable. A lover of music, he composed both classical ragas and folk songs. In numerous villages and towns surrounding Salon, many of the songs sung at the time of birth, marriage or festivity have been composed by Shah Naim Ata. A host of qawwals and a group of folk singers known as mirasins trained under him and many landed or talukadar families of the area retain these mirasins as their family singers. During my childhood, one such mirasin, Aseemun, was part of every ceremony or festivity that I travelled to attend in Lucknow or Mustafabad village. When I began working on this book, a now aged Aseemun had come to my parents' home (in her last years she travelled seeking help from the families she was attached to) and stayed for some days. I have this quote down from her in an old notebook: 'Shah Naim's compositions were for the people, regardless of their religion. There was no Hindu or Muslim.'

The words and tunes of Shah Naim Ata's songs are completely rooted in the region and vividly describe the sights and sounds of Awadh. While many dargahs are popular with non-Muslims because of their faith in the healing powers of Sufis' tombs, there are no such superstitions attached to the Salon shrine. Instead, this dargah is known for its contribution to the local indigenous culture of the region. Shah Naim Ata's grandson, Saiyid Zaheer Husain Jafri, is a historian. In a paper submitted to the Indian History Congress, titled *Landed Properties of a Sufi Establishment—a Study of Seventeenth and Nineteenth Century Documents from Salon in Awadh*, he writes about his ancestors distancing themselves from the orthodox Wahabi Muslims and having close links with non-Muslim followers: 'The keeper of the establishment did not have any sympathy for the religious zeal of the Wahabis under Saiyid Ahmad of Rae Bareli, who was told by the Sajjada Nashin and the zamindar of the area that they considered aiding the poor as more pious than indulging in a holy war.'

It is institutions such as the Salon shrine that play a key role in forging links between Hindus and Muslims at the popular level. They continue to be islands of serenity, even though the area has witnessed a communal assault launched by the Hindutva forces in the 1990s. Like the Salon dargah, there are numerous other Sufi shrines scattered across UP that have played a key role in the evolution of the local folk literature and music, and I believe this is also a strain in local culture that eventually expels fundamentalist forces. These are traditions that transcend religious boundaries and remain neither Hindu nor Muslim. They just epitomize a rich cultural landscape.

OF HUMANS AND CATTLE
Uttar Pradesh

A qawwali in the Awadhi dialect in praise of a Sufi named Haji Waris Ali Shah, describes the saint's early life by drawing a parallel with the childhood of Lord Krishna. The opening stanza of the qawwali goes:

> *Deva dasi Kunwar Kanhaiya,*
> *Mohan pyare bansi dhari,*
> *Janam ke raja,*
> *Sunder chaila Shyam behari.*

I hear this qawwali at the imposing marble mausoleum of Waris Shah in the small township of Deva on the outskirts of Lucknow. The cult of Waris Shah stands testament to the nature of Indian Islam. Waris Shah was an immensely popular Sufi who died as recently as 1905. He proclaimed the equality of all faiths, saying: 'Rise above all boundaries of race and religion, for he who is Rab is also Rama.' Thousands of Hindus were drawn to his fold and, even today, over half the worshippers at Deva Sharif are non-Muslims. There is even a belief that he met Sai Baba at some point and influenced him deeply. The great geographical distance between the abodes of Waris Ali Shah and Sai Baba would suggest this is unlikely, yet the legend persists.

Historians inform us that it was Sufis like Waris Shah who brought Islam to the masses. Most of the large-scale conversions in the subcontinent took place as communities and individuals came under the spell of the Islamic mystics who stressed the humane aspects of Islam. Their religious message was simple—belief in one God and the equality of all human beings—a message that held great appeal for a caste-oppressed society. There are numerous instances of entire communities and villages coming under the influence of a particular saint and converting to Islam to escape their caste-determined status.

The Islam preached by the Sufis was a liberal faith that accommodated many of the old beliefs and superstitions of the converts; that is why individuals like Sai Baba and Waris Ali appeal to non-Muslims. While Sai Baba is now a tradition managed and controlled by non-Muslims, Deva Sharif is popular with both faiths. Many of the rituals practiced in the Sufi dargahs in India are clearly Hindu in origin and are not found anywhere else in the Muslim world. Pilgrimages to shrines of saints, giving offerings and making vows, burning chirag and incense over the tomb of a saint, partaking of sweets and food given as offerings at the shrines as sacred portions, circumambulation of the shrine, touching relics of the departed saint and the general belief in their healing effect are not indigenous to Islam but a result of local belief systems. Even the practice of worshipping saints by giving them a divine status and attributing magical powers to their tombs is clearly inspired by Hindu devotionalism.

It is precisely for this reason that the Muslim orthodoxy had launched numerous campaigns to 'cleanse' Sufism from what they perceived to be 'impurities'. One of the biggest grounds that the reformers found for the condemnation of such cults was the resemblance to the practice of idol worship of the Hindus. One well-known book upholding this view is *Studies in Islamic Culture in the Indian Environment* by Aziz Ahmad. This scholar attacks the Sufi cult, saying: 'This is a general weakness which new converts to Islam, especially in India, introduce into its faith and practice... Tomb worship in India is an evil parallel to Hindu idolatory and borrowed by the Muslims because of their contact with the Hindus.'

As veneration of saints and their tombs was one of the most powerful religious-cultural bonds between Hindus and Muslims, any movement that denigrated these traditions was bound to put pressure on, and in some cases, debase these integrative mechanisms. Though these reformist purges did succeed in making many Muslims self-conscious about their religious practices, these syncretic traditions could not be altogether eliminated from Indian Islam. In many parts of the country, it is still the mazhaars and not the masjids that continue to exert the maximum pull on the Muslim masses. The fact that these traditions still survive despite decades of reformist campaigns, clearly underlines their strength and vitality. If the orthodoxy has not been able to wean people away from the Sufi cults, it is largely because the Sufis were the main vehicle for conversion in the subcontinent.

Thousands of Hindus, too, are drawn to the Sufi shrines largely because of their belief in the magical powers of the saints' tombs. In many cases, it is the Hindu patronage that accounts for a dargah's popularity and prosperity. At Deva Sharif, for instance, the biggest donor is a Hindu Rajput lady from Ajmer who visits the dargah every second month. Both Hindus and Muslims who have joined the order founded by Waris Shah, and live together within the dargah complex. They wear yellow robes and lead a life of celibacy. Naresh Singh is a Bhumihar from Bihar who became a follower of Waris Shah over a decade ago. Recently, he decided to become a regular inmate and take the vows of celibacy. Says he: 'Just because I have devoted my life to the saint does not mean that I am no longer a Hindu. Waris Shah used to say all religions are equal and none can claim to be better than the other. Waris Shah took part in Hindu festivals like Diwali though he was a Muslim. I am only following his example.' One of the biggest rural fairs takes place at Deva Sharif every year, which attracts both Hindu and Muslim performers. This fair is a mêlèe of folk forms such as dancing, folk singing, kavi sammelans, nautankis, qawwalis and mushairas. The structure itself is made of white marble and looks quite impressive.

Similarly, one of the biggest cattle fairs in the country is held at the mazhaar of Shah Madar in Makkanpur village of Kanpur district. Most of the cattle breeders, camel owners and horse trainers who crowd the fair are Hindus. But they consider

Shah Madar as their patron saint—each year they travel hundreds of miles to this dusty little town in North India to seek his blessing. It is also an occasion to do brisk business by selling livestock and cattle to wholesale traders. Faith and business merge happily in the chaos and anarchy of the huge congregation of humans and cattle. Nath Ram, a camel trader from Jaisalmer explained: 'It is auspicious to take the saint's blessings at least once a year. My community has been worshipping Shah Madar for generations now. For me, he is as important as Krishna or Rama.'

Both Makkanpur and Deva Sharif are important centres of popular Islam. The religion they advocate underlines the local roots of this country's Muslims.

PLATFORM PIRS
Uttar Pradesh

Lucknow and Aligarh are both cities with strong Muslim associations. The decaying but fabulous monuments of Lucknow stand testament to the city's nawabi lineage. And the Aligarh Muslim University remains the centrepiece of that township. But while the monuments of Lucknow are visited only by stray tourists and the Aligarh Muslim University empties out by late afternoon, there are two unknown shrines in both cities that draw long queues of worshippers, more Hindus than Muslims, every Thursday evening.

They are the abodes of the 'platform' Pirs. In Lucknow, this Pir is known as Khamman Pir. His medium-sized mazhaar lies between two platforms in the crowded Char Bagh station. The shrine was built just twenty-five years ago, before which there was only an unmarked grave at the site.

In Aligarh, the platform Pir is known as Baba Barchi Bahadur. His mazhaar is situated alongside a railway line near the entrance of the station. Till as recently as 1960, a tiny shrine under a neem tree denoted Barchi Bahadur's grave. In less than twenty-five years, this has become one of the most popular mazhaars of Aligarh.

The histories of both Khamman Pir and Barchi Bahadur are more the stuff of popular lore than hard facts. There is no historical evidence backing the existence of either Pir. Yet, at their dargahs, the caretakers and followers will recount colourful tales about both men's lives and exploits.

The most popular tale about Khamman Pir goes back to the days when the British were laying the first railway lines in Lucknow. Legend has it, that when the British tried to lay a track over the grave, they encountered the full wrath of the dead Pir. By day, the British would lay the line, and by night it would be uprooted. This went on for many days after which the British relented, begged for forgiveness at the grave and then laid the railway line skirting the site.

An identical legend is recounted by the followers of Barchi Bahadur at Aligarh. Barchi Bahadur's rise in popularity is attributed to the attachment of one Hazrat Zorar Hussain, who began constructing the shrine, and after his death in 1973, was buried alongside Barchi Bahadur. Twenty years hence, he also appears to have attained sainthood; his Urs is also celebrated.

In this manner, popular religion continues to create its saints and cults. Take the Khamman Pir phenomenon. Residents of the station area in Lucknow will tell you that the shrine has steadily grown in popularity over the last decade. And this popularity is largely due to Hindu attendance. Muslim worshippers are far fewer in numbers. Visit the dargah on any Thursday evening when long queues of devotees wait for at least an hour before making their offerings at the grave, and one will see that less than five per cent are Muslims.

In Lucknow, Khamman Pir is considered the patron saint of coolies, platform vendors, rickshaw pullers, tempo drivers and engine drivers. Trains slow down when they near the shrine and engine drivers bow their heads in reverence. Khamman Pir, they say, ensures a safe journey. 'If I don't show him respect, I increase the chances of meeting with an accident,' an engine driver told me.

But even more importantly, the shrine is known for its healing powers. And it is not just the unlettered who seek the Pir's blessings. V. Srivastava, a senior statistical officer in the State government, has been visiting the dargah for the last three years because he believes that the Pir cured his spondylitis. But it was Ram Avtar, a daily wage earner, who most succinctly summed up the reasons for visiting the shrine: 'Who has the money to visit a doctor? And if I go to a government hospital I will spend the whole day there and lose out on my daily earning. Then my family would starve and more people will fall sick. So each time any of us are ill, we come here, pray to Khamman Pir, feel a sense of peace, and hope that our illness will soon go away.'

The Khamman Pir phenomenon represents a popular brand of Sufism, which survives because of people's need for wish fulfilment and some comfort from the rigours of life. This type of Sufism is not woven through a religious order nor through language, music, literature or enlightened thinking, but through a common need for comfort and a place to go to seek it.

There is the flip side to the phenomena of platform and roadside Pirs and in other instances, temples. As nothing can be as easily exploited as superstitions, many racketeers build makeshift mazhaars on old abandoned graves to occupy land and supplement their incomes. In the middle-class locality of Nirala Nagar in Lucknow itself, a vegetable vendor has occupied a piece of land by claiming that a grave there belongs to a Pir baba. Residents claim that he began organizing qawwalis there some five years ago to strengthen his claim to the plot. Since then, small crowds have been gathering at the site and making offerings. It is quite possible that the platform Pir legend has been created to control a piece of real estate.

The vendor no longer sells vegetables. Peddling religion has proved to be more profitable.

A FAIR VIEW
Meerut, Uttar Pradesh

Meerut is often remembered for the vicious communal riots that engulfed the city in 1987. Since then, it has been listed as one of the most communally sensitive towns in North India, where a curfew is imposed at the slightest provocation. But visit this bustling industrial township of western Uttar Pradesh, just 60 kilometres from Delhi, and many old residents of Meerut, both Hindus and Muslims, will tell you that if the 1987 riots are Meerut's shame, the city's pride is the ongoing Nauchandi Mela. A bustling small town mela, it has evolved over the years into a very commercial event, but its origins lie in a great act of cooperation between the religious groups.

The mela commemorates both the Navratri celebration at the Chandi Devi Temple and the Urs festivity at a dargah known as Balley Mian's mazhaar. Every year, this month-long fair begins on the second Sunday after Holi—Navratri always falls during this period, as does the Urs of Balley Mian. One of the largest fairs in North India, the Nauchandi Mela is usually inaugurated by the district magistrate who performs puja at the temple and then offers a chaddar at the dargah. The mandir and the mazhaar are located opposite each other.

The ritual over, the mela then offers every conceivable form of entertainment—a circus, rides, musical shows, dance-drama, folk theatre, film shows, exhibitions and a variety of games. Given Meerut's history and location, there has been the odd year when few visitors would arrive. J. Sharma, a local advocate who was on the mela management committee, said that business was particularly slack during the period of communal tension in the late 1980s and early 1990s. The first time I visited the mela in 1993, only about half the usual crowd had turned up. That year, Sharma had told me: 'As you can see, some of the stalls are empty as many traders and artisans have also stayed away. People are afraid to come because of the tense atmosphere in the country after the Babri Masjid demolition. On most years, you will find people from all parts of North India visiting the mela.'

When I returned in 2012, it had just become a commercial tamasha, with companies sponsoring several stalls. It was as if Meerut had, for a while, forgotten the orgy of hatred. The qawwalis sung at Balley Mian's mazhaar mingled with the incessant clang of temple bells at the Chandi Devi Temple. Representatives of both shrines participated in each other's festivities; offerings from the mazhaar were sent to the mandir and vice versa. One of the worshippers at the dargah told me: 'We always invite people from the mandir for every function at the dargah. These two shrines represent the long friendship between the Hindus and Muslims of Meerut.'

The Nauchandi Mela gets its name from the Navratri celebration at the Chandi Devi Temple. But it is significant that one of the most important festive days at the mazhaar is also known as Nauchandi Jumerat. Jumerat, or Thursday evening, is considered auspicious at dargahs throughout the country and Nauchandi Jumerat is the Thursday night when the Urs celebration at Balley Mian's mazhaar begins. Muslims throughout Uttar Pradesh attach significance to Nauchandi Jumerat and most dargahs in the State organize special festivities on this date. Few Muslims are, however, aware that the term Nauchandi Jumerat is derived from the Goddess Chandi and that the tradition of considering this an auspicious day has its origins in the tiny dargah of Balley Mian in Meerut.

Balley Mian is, in fact, the local name of Sayyid Salar Masud Ghazi, one of the most popular Sufis of Uttar Pradesh, whose main shrine is in Bahraich, over 120 kilometres from Lucknow. The legend of Salar Masud Ghazi or Ghazi Miyan is a mix of fact and fiction. In an article on the Bahraich shrine, Dr Tahir Mehmood traces the most widely believed version of Ghazi Miyan's life. Ghazi Miyan was the nephew of Sultan Mahmud Ghaznavi, who accompanied his uncle on the military expedition to India in the early eleventh century. After the infamous sack of the Somnath mandir, he is believed to have become disillusioned with war and decided to devote himself to spreading the message of universal brotherhood and to the service of God and humanity. Ghazi Miyan is also believed to have rejected the throne of Delhi after conquering it. He then passed through Meerut, Kannauj, Malihabad and Satrikh before settling in the jungles surrounding Bahraich. He soon began to attract large crowds and became a sought after spiritual teacher. He tried to stop the practice of human sacrifice in the local temples and the exploitation of the poor by their rulers. This led to a direct conflict with the local rulers, who united against the leadership of one Raja Sahar Dev and put together an army to oust Ghazi Miyan. After a number of wars much against his will, the Ghazi finally fell defending his beliefs.

He was buried under the mahwa tree where he used to preach, and the local people, Hindus and Muslims alike, began to worship the spot. His grave was later rebuilt by a Hindu milkman whose wife was blessed with a child after praying to Ghazi Miyan. About thirty years after the saint's death, Zahra Bibi, the blind daughter of a local ruler, who regained her sight on praying to the Ghazi, constructed a magnificent tomb over the grave.

Legend has it, that while passing through Meerut, the Ghazi was injured and a part of his body fell on the spot where the Balley Mian mazhaar now stands. Emperor Qutubuddin Aibak is believed to have constructed this shrine and, according to information pieced together from local authorities and records, the Nauchandi Mela precedes the construction of the mazhaar. Earlier, it used to be a nine-day fair celebrating Navratri at the Chandi Devi Temple. But after the dargah was built, the Urs also began to be celebrated around the same time and the mela was gradually extended to an entire month.

Today, the people of Meerut are justifiably proud of this fair. Said Shabbir Ahmad, who had set up a food stall near the mandir-mazhaar complex: 'This proves that Hindus and Muslims of Meerut have had excellent relations in the past. Even now, we do this together to work for peace. Outsiders may think that the Hindus and Muslims of Meerut are completely divided. But the truth is that relations are normal unless politicians and goondas create trouble.' Santosh Mehta, a young lawyer, echoed these sentiments: 'This fair is the showpiece of Meerut. The city's municipality has even brought out an entire publication on the fair. We want to be remembered, not for communal bloodletting, but for promoting harmony.'

A young poet named Onkar Gulshan has penned a poem in Hindi on the fair titled 'Shahar ki hai shaan Nauchandi' (The pride of the city is Nauchandi). Some lines from the poem read as follows:

> *Mukhans maqbara Balley Mian aur Bhagwati mandir,*
> *Hai quami ekta ki dekhiye pehchaan Nauchandi.*
> *Kisi mazhab, kisi quam me antar nahi karti;*
> *Samajhti hai fakat insaan ko insaan Nauchandi...*

The shrine of Balley Mian and the Bhagwati Temple,
Communal parity is represented by Nauchandi.
It does not differentiate between communities;
All men are equal at Nauchandi...

The cynics might dismiss this fair as a mere showpiece that belies the reality on the ground; an empty symbolic gesture that camouflages the truth. But even if it's just a symbol, the Nauchandi Mela is surely the kind of symbol we must celebrate.

THE DIVISIONS AND THE POETS
Uttar Pradesh

The State of Uttar Pradesh is littered with any number of shrines, monuments, folklore and tradition, where people belonging to different castes and communities have contributed towards the evolution of a common culture. For instance, in Ayodhya itself, there is the Satyar Mandir, a temple dedicated to religious harmony, where idols of Rama and Krishna stand alongside Buddha, Mahavira, Christ and Zoroaster and are flanked on both sides by pictures of Mecca and Medina. In Bareilly, there is a temple known as Chunnu Mian's Mandir built by a Muslim of the same name. There are numerous dargahs scattered across the State that are considered sacred by Hindus and Muslims alike—Deva Sharif, Khamman Pir in Lucknow, Shah Madar in Makkanpur, Sayyid Salar Masud Ghazi's mazhaar in Bahraich, Salim Chishti in Agra. The list is long, extending across every little town and kasbah in a State that is bigger than most nations.

The period of British rule saw the beginnings of communal friction in the Gangetic belt. There are numerous reasons for this, but having a particularly potent impact on some of the areas that today comprise Uttar Pradesh were the religio-revivalist movements, both among the Hindus and the Muslims. The late nineteenth century saw the emergence of the Arya Samaj as a powerful force, the cow-protection movement and a campaign for the use of the Nagri script—all signs of a new Hindu consciousness.

A similar consciousness was seen in the Muslim community as well. In the Indian subcontinent, Muslim conversion has always taken numerous shapes. Some held on to 'pure' beliefs, but most converts who carried their pre-Islamic traditions into Islam were made increasingly aware of what were perceived to be the 'correct' practices. Inspired by Shah Waliullah of Delhi (1703-63) and Syed Ahmed Barelvi (1782-1832), many Muslim leaders, including those from the legendary seminary at Deoband in UP's Muzaffarnagar district, began to insist on a revitalized Muslim identity and 'purification' of Islam. This naturally amounted to an attack on syncretic forms of religious practice and Islam's local roots.

If the religio-revivalist movements weakened the secularist traditions in the State, subsequent political developments fuelled communalism in the area. Events in UP have always tended to cause a fall-out throughout the country. For instance, even after 1857, when the last vestiges of Muslim political power crumbled before the British, the Muslims of the United Provinces continued to be an affluent community who, besides cornering many government jobs, owned a disproportionate share of the land. It was eventually the landed aristocracy of this region that spearheaded the demand for Pakistan and made up the frontline leadership of the Muslim League, underlining the State's importance in shaping the destiny of the subcontinent.

Contemporary events have been heavily influenced by this history. Post-Partition, there has been a steady deterioration in the position of the State's Muslims. The division of the subcontinent saw the large-scale immigration of the Muslim elite and professionals to Pakistan, and the subsequent abolishing of the zamindari system in India completed the process of impoverishment of the Muslim elite and middle class. Today, many Muslims live in overcrowded city ghettos where unemployment and crime are rampant. Ironically, politics in the late 1980s and 1990s took such a turn in the crucible of this State, that this steadily impoverished community was accused of being pampered and 'appeased'. When the Ayodhya movement changed the political climate of India, it was in Uttar Pradesh that Muslims bore the brunt of communal violence.

The divisions and ghettoization of the mind is an ongoing process, although the political power of the Hindutva forces has been thwarted by caste-based parties. The State has all the realities: if a composite culture has thrived in the region today called Uttar Pradesh, it is also the breeding ground for religious revivalism and communalism. The whole issue of syncretism and communalism is far more complex in UP than in the more culturally homogenous states such as Kerala, Tamil Nadu or even West Bengal. If language binds the Hindus and

Muslims of the latter State (Rabindranath Tagore has authored the national anthems of both India and Bangladesh), in UP, the Hindi-Urdu issue has historically been effectively used to drive a wedge between the two communities.

It is necessary to revert to history to explain the realities in this State. But this is still a journalist's take on a region that I perhaps know best, outside of Delhi. The plains of Uttar Pradesh were the cradle of the ancient Vedic civilization. Some of the holiest Hindu pilgrimage centres lie within it—Mathura, Varanasi, Ayodhya, Kedarnath, Badrinath, Rishikesh, Hardwar—while the hills have now been carved into the separate State of Uttarakhand. It was in this very area that Muslim political power reached its zenith, particularly in the case of the Awadhi nawabs, who continued to be influential entities till 1857. Some of the great cities of the State came up under Muslim patronage—Agra, Lucknow, Jaunpur, Faizabad, to name just a few. The interaction with Islam, therefore, influenced every facet of civilization in the area—language, literature, folk traditions, architecture and even religious traditions.

And the Muslims never formed some exclusive 'foreign' entity. Aside from the fact that their own social, cultural and religious practices were cast in an indigenous mould, there were some enormously talented personalities who epitomized this. For instance, take the sixteenth-century poet Raskhan who became a Krishna devotee and is considered one of the masters of Braj Bhasha, which has had a rich literary tradition before Hindi. The pen name 'rasa', is described by one scholar as a Braj Bhasha pun, meaning 'mine of rasa'. Born Saiyad Ibrahim, the son of a minor jagirdar, he moved to Vrindavan after becoming a Krishna bhakt. He composed a rich body of devotional poems describing the beauty of Krishna and his love for Radha. His leelas or devotional songs on Krishna are still popular and anyone who follows the evolution of Braj and Hindi, is familiar with his works, still available most commonly as *Raskhan Rachnavali*. His grave at Mahavan in Mathura, is a popular pilgrimage spot.

If Braj Bhasha was nurtured by Raskhan, one of the greatest works in Awadhi is undoubtedly Malik Mohammad Jaisi's epic poem, *Padmavat*. Born in Jais in what is now the Rae Bareli district, he died in 1542 and is buried in Ram Nagar near Amethi. The poet's own life is believed to have been fascinating, a saga of personal loss, that culminated in him joining the wandering Sufis. The *Padmavat* is an extraordinary work that explores the nature of physical and spiritual love, etches out the personalities of two strong women, the beautiful Padmavati and Nagmati, and also tells of the siege of Chittor by Alauddin Khilji. It is often described as a sacred love poem that explores the human affliction of love and the search for spirituality and truth. Many deem it to be an unparalled piece of writing and the first epic poem in a Hindi dialect. The other major work in Awadhi from the same period is Tulsidas's *Ramcharitmanas*.

In a much later era than Raskhan and Jaisi, we have the eighteenth-century poet Nazir Akbarabadi, who is seen as the consummate people's poet—irreverent, funny, writing on life and inanimate objects, serious poetry on poverty and the human condition, and verses on Hindu divinities and festivals.

He too, along with several other Urdu poets, stands testimony to the remarkable inter-religious mingling that took place at various points of the region's history.

Let me put forward the provocative statement that even the authors of the Hindutva agitation have picked up elements from Islamic models, particularly in Uttar Pradesh. The visible forms of the Ayodhya agitation—marching in processions, expressing the willingness to 'die' for the temple, asking people to turn towards Ayodhya at a particular time—are clearly borrowed from Islamic practice. As I examined religious forms and rituals, I was convinced that the votaries of Hindutva have borrowed liberally from forms of Islamic organizations to give their religious identity a more aggressive edge. As for the fused cultural identities of the region, the advocates of Puritanism on both sides prefer a more arid landscape.

RHYTHM OF THE BRAHMAPUTRA
Hajo, Assam

I do not make any distinction between
a Hindu and a Muslim, O Allah.
When dead, a Hindu will be cremated by fire,
while a Muslim will be buried under the same earth.

—a zikir composed by Azan Fakir,
a seventeenth-century saint from Assam.

As in other parts of the country, the gap between Hindus and Muslims appears to be widening in Assam as well. But here, it is the large-scale migration of Bengali Muslims, and not the Babri Masjid demolition and subsequent politics of identity, which has driven a wedge between the two communities. The Hindu-Muslim divide is superseded by the Assamese-Bengali divide and assertions of the ethnic distinctiveness of various tribal groups.

But there are traditions that endure between the two dominant religions in the State—particularly among the Assamese, who have a long tradition of close inter-community relations—that defy social tensions and political agendas. The language, dress and food habits of the Assamese Hindus and Muslims are virtually identical and they even celebrate common festivals like Bihu. But perhaps the most abiding symbols of Hindu-Muslim synthesis in the State are the zikirs (short devotional songs) composed by Azan Fakir in Assamese. Shah Milan, who later came to be called Azan Fakir, is generally believed to have come to India from Baghdad. After stopping at Ajmer and Delhi, where he was initiated into the Chishti order, he set off for Assam. The Sufi saint's first stop in Assam was the tomb of Ghyasuddin Auliya in Hajo, near Guwahati. He is supposed to have spent considerable time there mastering the Assamese language. From Hajo, he went to Gargaon, the capital of the Ahom kingdom. The Ahom king is believed to have accorded him a warm reception and given him some land near Sibsagar where he eventually settled down after marrying a local Ahom woman. His mazhaar now stands on the confluence of two rivers in Saraguri Chapari village in Sibsagar district.

Azan Fakir composed hundreds of zikirs—derived from the Arabic word 'ziqr' which means 'remembering Allah's name'—in Assamese. Though the main purpose of zikirs was to spread the message of Islam, what is remarkable about these compositions is that they are closely modelled on local folk songs known as Deh Bicarer Geet and the devotional songs of the Vaishnav Hindus. Moreover, though Azan Fakir was a devout Muslim, he respected all religions, and many of the zikirs are secular in character. Take the following composition for instance:

> *The Quran and Puranas teach the same thing;*
> *Understand O Mahatma,*
> *That for the wise man,*
> *Different scriptures preach the same truth.*

These lines reveal that Azan Fakir encouraged the incantation of God's name, which was also the essence of the Vaishnavism preached by Sankardeva, the great Bhakti reformer of Assam. Like Islam, the Namdharma propagated by Sankardeva—which is today, the dominant Hindu cult in Assam—was also against idol worship. The stress was on the japa (chanting) of God's naam or name. That is why some scholars argue that the Islam preached by Azan Fakir was compatible with the dominant Vaishnav faith of the region. Though dancing is generally considered a taboo for Muslims, Azan Fakir knew that the zikirs would lose much of their rhythmic tempo and attraction if dancing were to be banned as the locals were used to dancing and music. It is, therefore, common to see Assamese Muslims dancing to the zikirs.

The zikirs are undoubtedly an attempt at the synthesis of Islamic and Hindu ideals and motifs. Many of the compositions use Hindu imagery when they refer to the harp of Kailasa or to Sankar Deva and Madhava Deva, another great Bhakti reformer. In some zikirs, later composed by others, even Azan Pir is referred to as Azan Deva Fakir.

Much of the work on Azan Fakir has been done by Syed Abdul Malik, the well-known Assamese writer, who has won both the Padma Shri and the Padma Bhushan for his contribution to the language. In 1952, Guwahati University asked Malik to research the saint and collect all his surviving zikirs. Malik eventually published his collection of zikirs in an Assamese book. When I went to meet Malik in his Jorhat home in 1993, he explained: 'The zikirs are a perfect blend of Islamic and Hindu ideals. Today, in particular, they are being revived as they are considered a symbol of Hindu-Muslim synthesis and unity. Just as the tunes and structure of the zikirs are based on the Vaishnav Kavyas, the zikir dance is also adapted from local folk forms. Though traditionally they are sung at ceremonies and functions at Muslim homes, today zikirs are increasingly sung at public functions and are also taught in schools and colleges.'

If Azan Fakir had based his zikirs on Vaishnav songs, Abdul Malik had gone down the same path and written an entire book on the life of Sankardeva. He claimed that his bestselling book, *Dhanya Nara Tanu Bhaal* has sold a record 30,000 copies and is kept in many nam ghars, the main centres of Vaishnav worship. He told me: 'This is the tradition of Assam. Here, I, a Muslim, have written a major work on the most important Hindu saint, Sankardeva. Similarly, some of the earliest books in Assamese on the life of Prophet Mohammad have been written by non-Muslims.' Abdul Malik passed away in 2000 at the age of eighty-one.

He is considered a doyen of Assamese writing. He wrote sixty novels, five collections of poems, five books for children, three travelogues and 3000 short stories. In 2009, a statue of Malik was unveiled at Golaghat, where he was born. Much of his fiction has romantic themes, but there is a body of work dealing with social issues. When I met him, he said he was most proud of his monumental collection of zikirs and songs of Azan Fakir. He believed he was collecting the history of the State for its people.

In a sense, he was part of a tradition in Assam. The first book on Prophet Mohammad in Assamese was written by the well-known writer Mahadeb Sharma. Another early work on Prophet Mohammad was written by Gopinath Bordoloi, the legendary former chief minister of Assam. Writer Tarun Phukan was the first to translate the fateha of the Quran into Assamese verse. Similarly, one of the best-known short stories set in Assam titled 'Shiraz' tells the tale of a Muslim who married a Hindu widow and allowed her to continue practising her faith. The immortal little story was penned by Lakshmi Dhar Sharma.

This is the tradition the State inherits. Little wonder that the Assamese are cohesive and confident about their cultural identity, regardless of different religions. The divisions that have been played on by politicians are between the Assamese and the Bengali, and within that, the greater mobilization has been against Muslim migrants from Bangladesh. The script that has been written for the State is far removed from the zikirs composed three hundred years ago by a Muslim saint, whose call for a Hindu-Muslim synthesis seems almost naïve today.

TWO FAITHS, ONE HOUSE
Karnataka

A shrine can be the focus of dispute or a symbol of happy co-existence. The importance of places of worship should never be underestimated, given the fact that the Ayodhya movement became one of the pivots of political mobilization in recent Indian history. As the self-styled custodians of faith periodically mesmerize the nation by keeping the spotlight focused on such disputes, the many places of worship sacred to both Hindus and Muslims remain in the shadows.

For, not only have temples and mosques existed side by side for centuries, there are some shrines that exist as both a mandir and a mazhaar. The Tinthani Mouneshwar in Karnataka's Gulbarga district is one such shrine which Hindus consider a temple and Muslims, a dargah. And no, they are not fighting over it. Tinthani is a remote and tiny village in the Shorapur taluka of Gulbarga district, over 130 kilometres from the district headquarters. There was no pukkah road to the village when I first visited in 1993. It lay five kilometres off the national highway.

But having to walk this distance did not deter thousands of devotees from making their way to Tinthani every year to visit the shrine of Saint Mouneshwar on the banks of the river Krishna. Hindus called the shrine Mouneshwarji ka mandir, while Muslims called it Monappiah's dargah. It was effectively both: while puja took place before an image of the saint, just above the image was a tiny room that housed the grave or mazhaar. Shiv Shamkar, a regular devotee, told us: 'I come here every month from a village about 30 kilometres away. Though most of the devotees are Hindus, there are many Muslims as well. We have no problem worshipping side by side. Why should there be any difference between me and a Muslim worshipper when we have both come to pay our respects to Mouneshwar baba?'

The building itself was a fascinating blend of Islamic and Hindu styles and motifs. The main structure has a typically Islamic gumbaz (dome) flanked by minarets and lies at the centre of a vast courtyard. As is commonly found in dargahs, there were small rooms for pilgrims on both sides of the courtyard. From outside, the shrine looked like a typical masjid.

But as you walk up to the entrance, four huge temple bells greet you. After crossing the courtyard, a short flight of steps leads to the sanctum sanctorum. A picture of Mouneshwar baba hangs there; he is dressed like a sadhu and sits with his legs crossed in a yogic posture. All the paraphernalia necessary for puja is kept before the image. Just above the image is a small wooden door. One can reach the door by walking up the short flight of steps flanking the picture. Open the door and you will see a grave covered with a chaddar and a picture of

Mecca-Medina on the wall. This two-tier shrine functions as a temple on one level and as a dargah on another.

The management of the shrine is in the hands of the local administration that hires all the staff. The year I visited, I spoke to the manager and a watchman. Appropriately, Basoraja, the manager, was a Hindu while the watchman that year was Badshah Sahib, a Muslim. Besides, there were two pujaris, Gangadas Swami and Shiv Shankar, who lived in an impressive house next to the shrine. This pujari told us: 'We have never discriminated between Hindus and Muslims. If I have a home today, it is because I have the blessings of both communities.'

An annual fair is held here for fifteen days in January-February. For Muslims, this is the Urs while Hindus call it the Jatra. Subhash Rao, a teacher at the local school in Tinthani explained: 'During the Jatra, we follow both the Hindu custom of offering puja and the Islamic tradition of putting a chaddar (locally called a 'gillof') on the grave. Thousands crowd Tinthani during the Jatra and devotees wait for several hours to have darshan of Mouneshwar baba.' Said Rahim Khan, a trader from a neighbouring village: 'The Jatra is one of the most exciting events in this region. Hindu and Muslim traders set up stalls side by side. We make no difference between the two communities. All are the children of God. This is the message of our saint.'

Who exactly was Mouneshwar? A brief entry in the Gulbarga district census handbook says that he was a Hindu saint who was attracted to many Sufi ideals. 'Though of the Viswakarma caste by birth, he was greatly attracted to the tenets of Islam.

His famous tomb at Tinthani is thus an object of worship for the Muslims as well as the Hindus,' records the book without mentioning any dates.

The legends about this saint are far more colourful. One of the most popular tales in the region describes Mouneshwar performing a miracle for a Muslim nobleman from Bijapur. This nobleman eventually became the saint's most devoted follower, and strangely enough, took on the name of Mohammad Paigambar. As is often the case with popular religion, the cult of Mouneshwar too, is made up of entertaining, unrealistic legends that often defy all logic. All the same, it is one of the best examples of a popular composite culture existing at the grassroots level in upper Karnataka.

Though the life and teachings of Mouneshwar appear to have eluded serious academic scrutiny, the Tinthani Mouneshwar is no insignificant village shrine. On the contrary, this is one of the most popular religious cults in the Gulbarga region. Though primarily a rural cult, there are some devotees who come all the way from cities like Hyderabad, Bijapur and even Mumbai to pay homage to the saint. According to the district commissioner of Gulbarga, during the Jatra, the administration works day and night to cater to the endless stream of pilgrims.

Despite the lack of research into the cult, one can clearly see the synthesis of Sufi and Bhakti ideals in the figure of Mouneshwar. The Gulbarga-Bijapur belt was an important centre for both the Bhakti and the Sufi movements in the Deccan. Sufis belonging to every conceivable order had settled in the region when it was the seat of Muslim power and the towns and villages are still dotted with their mazhaars. Moreover, the most famous Sufi of the Deccan, Bandanawaz Gesudaraz, had also settled in Gulbarga and his magnificent tomb is still the pride of the town.

Similarly, the most powerful Bhakti movement in Karnataka also began in the Gulbarga-Bijapur belt. A reformer named Basava, whose samadhi stands in the heart of Gulbarga, is credited with initiating the Lingayat Bhakti movement. Basava rejected caste, Brahmanical rituals, polytheism and even the authority of Vedic texts. In their place, he declared the Lingayat creed open to all and only demanded devotion to Lord Shiva. Despite the egalitarian nature of Lingayat Bhakti, social distinctions gradually crept into the movement and today the Lingayats have transformed from a sect to one of the most powerful castes in Karnataka.

The Bhakti movement in all parts of the country was essentially aimed at breaking Brahmanical control over religion. Reams have been written about the influence of Islamic egalitarianism and humanism on the Bhakti ideals of breaking caste barriers and making God accessible to all. There is little doubt that the Sufis and Bhaktas of the Deccan belt were also in constant touch with each other. Indeed, the Lingayats in particular appear to have been drawn to many Sufi institutions and ideals. In his classic work, *The Sufis of Bijapur*, R. M. Eaton writes: 'Apart from the doctrinal similarities between the Lingayat faith and Islam, specific Lingayat socio-religious institutions compare remarkably with that of the Sufis. The Math and the Khanqah both functioned as centres for spiritual guidance...while both the guru and the Pir initiated members into the spiritual fold and mediated between the devotee and the deity.'

The non-Muslim devotees at dargahs in upper Karnataka are often Lingayats. In many Sufi shrines, such as the tomb of Ahmad Shah Wali in Bidar, Lingayats even preside over the Urs ceremony. In fact, a recent Lingayat virakta (ascetic) was a Muslim who drew his followers from both the Lingayat and Muslim communities. This phenomenon of Lingayat devotionalism at Sufi centres is one of the most powerful integrative forces in northern Karnataka.

The cult of Mouneshwar represents the high point of this synthesis between Bhakti and Sufi ideals in the region. The close historical links between the Islamic mystics and the Hindu Bhaktas of upper Karnataka made it possible for such an unusual cult to strike deep roots and thrive. This little cult is, however, relatively unknown outside of the region. The believers come with faithful regularity but there is no knowledge about it outside. Those who worship here say they have a significant message to share with the country. As Yaqub, a trader in Tinthani, put it: 'Look how they fought over whether the Babri Masjid was a temple or a mosque. Here, in Tinthani, one building houses both a mandir and a dargah, and Hindus and Muslims worship together without any dispute.'

But the potential for a communal spark and a Hindu takeover is there with the BJP now a powerful force in Karnataka and the RSS active in the belt. This is just the sort of shrine that Hindus begin to claim as their own and Muslims slowly abandon for reasons as varied as succumbing to the dominant community and also propagating the conservative Islamic models that have no space for such beliefs.

THE MEITEI BOND
Manipur

Manipur is always in the news for the wrong reasons. There is the insurgency against the Indian State, Kuki-Naga clashes, and at times, even Hindu-Muslim violence. But few people outside the State are even remotely aware of who exactly the Kukis and Nagas are. Similarly, when this troubled State made headlines in Delhi dailies in May this year, it was because of communal violence which claimed the lives of about a hundred Manipuri Muslims. At that time, Delhi typically responded with complete surprise at the fact that there were Muslims in Manipur.

Although tiny, Manipur is an extremely complex State. Its people can be broadly classified into three major ethnic groups—the Meiteis, the Kukis and the Nagas. The Meiteis are by far the most dominant group, constituting over 60 per cent of the State's one and a half million people. Most Meiteis are Hindus who live in the 700 square miles of the Imphal valley. But about 9 per cent of Manipur's people are Meitei Muslims—a fact that few people outside the State know. While the Meiteis—both Hindus and Muslims—dominate the fertile Imphal valley, the surrounding hills are home to a bewildering number of tribes who constitute about 32 per cent of Manipur's population. It is these tribes that are broadly classified under two major groups—the Kukis and Nagas. About 80 per cent of these tribals are Christians. This minuscule State is, therefore, home to all the three major religions. The co-existence of these world religions with the original tribal values and customs makes Manipur a fascinating study.

Hinduism became a dominant force in Manipur in the eighteenth century when the king, Garib Niwas (1708-48), declared Vaishnavism as the official State religion. This was the Vaishnavism of Chaitanya Mahaprabhu, the great Bhakti preacher of Bengal, which stressed on Krishna bhakti. The embracing of Vaishnavism did not, however, imply that the old pre-Hindu animistic religion of the Meiteis, known as lais, was buried. Though some tribal customs such as human sacrifice were abandoned, in most instances, the old Meitei deities continued to be worshipped alongside the new Vaishnav gods. Till date, the traditional Meitei priests and priestesses, known as maibas and maibis, play a prominent role in the religious life of Manipur along with the Brahmins and Vaishnav priests. In a fascinating synthesis, some of the traditional Meitei gods have come to be identified with the new Hindu deities. Similarly, the Meiteis continue to celebrate their traditional festivals alongside Hindu festivals.

The most evolved expression of this fusion is, however, the Manipuri dance. Though the origins of this dance form lie in pre-Hindu tradition and customs, the dominant theme of most dance recitals today is the Radha-Krishna lore. The temple of Thangjing in Moirang town is the most popular pre-Hindu Meitei shrine, besides being a great centre of Manipuri dance. The ancient Meitei ritual of Lai Haraoba (the creation dance of the Meitei Thangjing Temple) stands testament to the catholicity and absorbing power of Hinduism.

Islam came to Manipur around the same time as Hinduism. The early seventeenth century saw the arrival of the first Muslims. Most of them were war captives as Muslim mercenaries had joined the armies of some kings who were defeated by the maharaja of Manipur. Some of the early Muslims were also artisans and gun makers who were brought to Manipur by the maharaja. All these Muslims eventually settled down in the State. They married local Meitei women and their descendants came to be known as Manipuri Muslims.

The enlightened policies of some Manipuri rulers like Garib Niwas helped the socialization process between Hindus and Muslims. In the course of time, the Muslims had been integrated into Manipuri society to such an extent that they were even given traditional Meitei clan names. Even today, Manipuri Muslims have clan names such as Ipham, Kulaibaum, Koijing, Wang, Bogi, Mogjai, Monam and Chesham. But the strongest bond linking the Hindus and Muslims of the valley is the Manipuri language. According to Janab Khan, a Manipuri Muslim scholar: 'We identify with every facet of Meitei culture—food, language, dress. Even our women are more advanced than Muslim women elsewhere. This is because women have always been strong in Manipur.'

The riots in May 2012 were, therefore, not a reflection of any Hindu-Muslim animosity or divide. To a large extent, they were a fallout of the spreading insurgency in the region. A Meitei insurgent group, People's Revolutionary Army (PRA), had a clash with a Muslim drug dealer. This minor scuffle eventually snowballed into a massacre—a hundred Muslims were killed while only three Hindus lost their lives. A local journalist told us: 'This was not a communal riot. Here, one group spread rumours about Muslims and went about killing them. Only after the storm had settled did we realize that it was a well-executed revenge of the Muslims by the PRA.'

The presence of numerous insurgent groups is also responsible for the ongoing Kuki-Naga clashes. Both sides are in the grip of separatist underground organizations that aspire for independent Kuki and Naga homelands. The most powerful group in the fray is the National Socialist Council of Nagaland (Muivah faction) which is spearheading a ruthless 'ethnic cleansing' of Kukis from Naga dominated areas. Kuki underground outfits such as the Kuki National Army and the Kuki Revolutionary Army are no match for the better-armed Nagas. Besides the traditional tribal hostility, the latest round of fighting is for land.

Though most Kukis and the Nagas are Christians, they have displayed little charity towards one another. On the contrary, the past year has seen the two groups engage in a ruthless warfare that has claimed almost three hundred lives.

150   *In Good Faith*

Internecine warfare, raids on neighbouring tribes and even headhunting, were part of the tribal way of life till early this century. British rule and the 'century of mission', which saw most tribals embrace Christianity, is believed to have transformed their lives. The greatest contribution of the missionaries was, however, their emphasis on education—the upshot is that, today the Northeastern states have the highest literacy in the country (56 per cent) after Kerala. However, the major contribution of Christianity has been that it has managed to help the tribals preserve a separate identity. In positive terms, it means that Christianity has served as a defence mechanism against loss of tribal identity by absorbing them into mainstream Hindu society. But seen from another angle, it has also kept them apart from the same society. As one Naga scholar puts it: 'If we had not become Christians, we would have been the lowest caste of Hindus in the region.'

The Kuki-Naga warfare proves that the Christian brotherhood can often cave in before tribal traditions of warfare. These clashes also underline that ethnic, linguistic and regional considerations often outweigh religion in defining a people's sensibility. In the case of the Northeast at least, tribal and clan loyalties easily transcend religious bonds. Yet as far as the Meiteis are concerned, there are bonds that have still not snapped across religious boundaries.

MISSION ACCOMPLISHED

To search for a composite culture in the Northeastern states of India is to begin on another journey to understand the impact of the Church. One of most fascinating examples of socio-religious change is the impact of Christianity on the tribal hill people of the Northeast. In just over a century, a majority of the tribals have abandoned their animistic faiths, and adopted Christianity. And perhaps the greatest gift of this faith has been that the spread of Christianity has gone hand in hand with the spread of literacy.

No student of Christianity would attempt to argue that the missionaries did not benefit from the policies of the British administration. In a paper titled *Social Formations in North East India*, Professor Annada C. Bhagabati writes: 'Spiritual gains apart, the success of conversion should also be seen in terms of the technology the missionaries involved for the well-being of the people. The development of written forms of various languages, printing of books (beginning with the Bible), medical work and opening of schools were but some of the major introductions into the tribal area.'

Today, there are no missionaries left in the Northeast. The church is now run by locals and western missionaries only visit briefly when they get a visa to travel to India. The Reverend of the Union Baptist Church in Kohima, Nagaland's capital, pointed out that the maximum number of conversions took place, not during British rule, but after independence. Till 1955, for instance, only 45 per cent of Nagas had adopted Christianity; today 95 per cent have. This is clearly linked to the material gains offered by the church. Spiritual quest is always linked to palpable material gains in the case of mass conversions, be it to Christianity or, in the medieval period, to Islam.

Many sociologists maintain that one of the functions of Christianity was to help the hill tribes preserve their identities against the perceived threat of assimilation into the lowest level of the Hindu societies of the plains. Simply put, this means that the tribals preferred adopting Christianity to being categorised as low-caste Hindus. In the process, Christianity also tended to reinforce the traditional animosity between the hill tribes and the people from the plains, adding to the isolation of the hill states from mainland India. Any visitor to the Northeast will realize that the inhabitants of the tiny hill states are almost obsessive about maintaining their distinct tribal identities.

It is always difficult to promote a particular identity without undermining a larger national identity, and this is precisely what has happened in the Northeast. All inhabitants of these states will identify themselves as Nagas or Mizos while they are quick to label the outsider as 'Indian'. It is because of this that the Church in the Northeast is often accused of fanning separatism. But here the point should be made that the so-called separatist tendencies amongst some of the tribes are attempts to redefine their socio-cultural identity vis-à-vis independent India, as for most tribals, the experience of being part of a larger nation is relatively recent. Moreover, as Niu, a Naga youth from the Angami tribe put it: 'Don't forget that our ethnic stock is different (Mongolian), our languages have no root in Sanskrit, and even our religion is different from Indians.'

While Christianity has indeed played a role in preserving a 'separate' tribal identity, this does not imply that the religion has also preserved the old tribal way of life. On the contrary, old tribal rituals have been forgotten, religious practices transformed, socio-economic linkages modified. There is, however, one wonderful tribal tradition that survives today—the lack of social stratification. While there are indeed the rich and the poor, this does not stop them from eating and drinking together. Servility is almost absent in the Northeast, as each man considers himself equal to the next. This tradition is obviously rooted in the old tribal custom of collective living. Combine this with high literacy levels and you have a collective of remarkably proud people.

Most Indians make much of the corruption and insurgencies plaguing the region. Few care to look deeper and extol the remarkable achievements of region that was the Indian equivalent of the Wild West till recently and is often still seen as such in mainstream India. Of a people who did not even have a written script till a century ago, but today, with a little help from the Church, have made themselves a part of the most literate people in India.

THE CONVERSION QUESTION

A leading daily in Delhi recently carried a report from a village in Tamil Nadu's Madurai district about low-caste Hindus converting to Islam. Headlined 'Caste oppression forcing Harijans to convert to Islam', the report claimed that out of the thousand Harijans of Kurayoor village, three hundred have converted to Islam since 1982 because of the 'humiliation of not being treated as equals'. Having said all this, the correspondent then claimed that 'the converts do not seem to have gained anything—neither social status nor Gulf jobs.' The converts are still addressed by their old caste names and 'the Muslims also do not treat the converts on par with them'.

Conversion has always been one of the more complex issues that require to be addressed tangentially in any work on syncretic traditions. If caste alone was the motivating factor for conversion to Islam, then logically all low castes should have embraced the faith. At the same time, the phenomenon of entire caste and/or occupational groups converting to Islam during the medieval period suggests that caste was indeed an impetus for conversion. The Sufis also played an important role in this process as there are numerous recorded instances of entire clans, villages or communities declaring themselves Muslims after coming under the influence of a particular Sufi order or saint. It was possibly these factors, combined with economic considerations that led to large-scale conversions at various periods in Indian history.

As for the recent conversions in Tamil Nadu (if indeed they have taken place), they, too, suggest that considerations other than the spiritual had motivated them to embrace Islam. In fact, the same news report also claims that two hundred Harijans of another village in Madurai district have threatened to convert to Islam on 15 August if the government does not settle a local dispute between them and some backward-caste villagers.

There is an irony in the entire process of low castes embracing Islam to escape social disadvantages, for, much against the ideal of Islamic egalitarianism, Indian Muslim society, too, is divided on caste lines. No Saiyyad from North India would marry a Julaha; just as in Tamil Nadu, the Maraikayar Muslims, who trace their lineage to the early Arab traders, consider themselves notches above the Labbais or later converts.

The evidence of entire occupational groups converting to Islam is, in fact, strengthened by the names of many of the so-called Muslim castes such as Nai, Kasai, Julaha or Darzi, but conversion has never implied an instant transformation or shedding of social baggage. On the contrary, it takes several generations for a discernible acceptance into mainstream

Muslim society. While conversions to Islam are today rare and far between, the Church has been far more effective in conversions through the nineteenth and twentieth centuries. In less than a hundred years, all the tribals of the Northeastern hill states like Mizoram, Nagaland and, to a lesser extent, Manipur and Meghalaya, have converted to Christianity. And in South India, the Church has long since been one of the catalysts for social change.

Like the preachers of early Islam, the early Christian missionaries in South India too found it difficult to break the caste and kinship ties of the converts. The Church found a way out of this by accepting the caste structure. This acceptance was followed by large-scale mass movements towards the Church among the ranks of the depressed classes in the latter half of the nineteenth century. This impressed upon the Church the usefulness of retaining the caste structure, thereby preserving, to an extent, the old caste and kinship ties between the converted and non-converted. The result is that South Indian Christians identify themselves as much by caste as by religion. The sustained campaign by Dalit Christians to get caste-based reservations in educational institutions and jobs is evidence of that. Then there is the other example of the Nadars, who consider their caste their most defining marker of identity and are often happy to intermarry between their Christian and Hindu members. As with Islam, the egalitarian ideals of Christianity, too, had to give way before the age-old divisions of caste.

Social legislation and the empowerment of people through a democratic system corrected many of the more dehumanizing aspects of the caste system. A mass movement towards embracing the Church, therefore, appears to have petered out in South India, although conversions continue. In pockets of tribal India and states such as Jharkhand, Chhattisgarh and parts of Orissa, conversions continue on a larger scale as people find educational possibilities and the sense of community improves; many still see the Church as a vehicle for improving their economic lot. In tribal pockets however, the Church is also countered by the VHP-RSS structure that runs a motivated and communally charged campaign against conversion, often resulting in terrible violence, such as the burning of the missionary Graham Staines and his two sons, and the attacks on Christians in Orissa. There are other little conflicts that continue in tribal interiors without drawing the attention of the State.

Yet, for many people at the bottom of the social scale, joining the Christian fold still means access to the many mission-run schools, better jobs and opportunities, as well as an organized manner to combat forces that always seek to encroach upon and exploit tribal lands and people. Besides, the statistics clearly reveal that the Christians do remarkable work in the field of education, even if their motive is simply to 'harvest souls'. Consider some of the evidence: the Northeastern states have high levels of literacy. And if Kottayam district of Kerala became the first fully literate district in the country, it was because it is Christian dominated and, therefore, had a head start in education.

The politics of conversion are, therefore, intrinsically linked to the politics of survival. In the complexities of contemporary

India, this creates several paradoxes. On the one hand, you have Muslim groups hankering to be declared scheduled castes or backwards in order to benefit from reservations. On the other hand, a group of Harijans threaten to convert to Islam if the government does not do their bidding. But as people shift religious identity, they carry some markers, abandon others, take old rituals into the new faith and actually transform it in their own way, a composite culture continues to evolve and change.

THE VIRGIN GUSHING MILK
Tamil Nadu

'Some time during the sixteenth century, Our Lady with her infant son appeared to a Hindu boy carrying milk to a customer's home. While he rested under a banyan tree under a tank, Our Lady appeared to him and asked for milk for her son and the boy gave her some. On reaching the customer's home, the boy apologized for his lateness and the reduced amount of milk by relating the incident that occurred on his way. On inspection, the man found the milk pot to be full and realized that something miraculous had happened. The man, also a Hindu, wanting to see the place where the apparition occurred, accompanied the boy. When they reached the tank, Our Lady appeared once again. On learning that it was Our Lady who appeared to the boy, the residents of the local Catholic community became ecstatic. The tank where the apparition took place is called "Matha Kulam" or "Our Lady's tank".'

This is the origin of the legend of the Vailankanni Church according to the website maintained by its management. It's a fabulous structure, a few miles from Nagapattinam on the Tanjore coast. The structure, also called the 'Lourdes of the East', came up after the Lady apparently saved Portuguese sailors from a violent sea storm, about five hundred years ago. Now known as the basilica of Our Lady of Good Health, the church attracts about two million pilgrims each year. The church itself is an imposing white building. Over the years, the Portuguese brought porcelain plates and other relics to the shrine. In 1771, Vailankanni acquired the status of a parish and in 1962, the church building was raised to the status of a basilica by Pope John Paul XXIII.

The main idol was a gift from the Portuguese. It is a statue of Mary holding her infant son and standing on a globe. But beyond that, the church has spawned a wholly indigenous cult. On the ten days of the annual festival, held between August and September, it sees all the local forms of worship, as Mass is conducted in at least eight languages—Tamil, Malayalam, Kannada, Telugu, Konkani, Hindi, Marathi and English. People from all religions and castes crowd the church now known for its miraculous powers of healing. Velli, from Kerala, offered her hair at the shrine after her father was cured of an immune disorder. She is a Hindu and sees the Vailankanni Virgin as a Shakti figure, an Amman goddess. Another group of pilgrims from Andhra Pradesh stayed in Vailankanni for a week, praying for the health of their families. They were practising Hindus, but an annual visit to the church was now part of their cycle of life.

In the legend of this Mary, she reveals herself through gushing milk and blood. According to historian Susan Bayly, who briefly mentions this church in *Saints, Goddesses and Kings*, 'This is a familiar motif in Tamil stalapurana (temple history).' She also observes that the oral versions of the Vailankanni legend connect the Virgin even more explicitly with the surrounding Hindu sacred landscape. 'Officials who conduct pilgrims around the site declare that the basilica was built on the site of an existing Amman temple. According to one published foundation account, the Virgin established herself at Vailankanni after triumphing in a bloody battle against the reigning Tamil goddess.'

To my mind, history only bears out what I observed at Vailankanni. This was the most dynamic cult worship in a church that I have ever witnessed in India. Here, there is a constant stream of worshippers prostrating before the Virgin, lying flat on their stomachs, moving inch by inch towards the statue. They are making offerings, chanting their own prayers, asking for spirits to be exorcized, seeking miraculous cures, lighting incense sticks and candles. In every sense, this was a church that was expanding its power, authority and popularity by accommodating every local custom and belief system. It was circumscribing nothing. Worshippers could see the Virgin as they chose to. They could worship as they chose to.

JOURNEY'S END

Kashmir

In Kashmir we can contemplate both the making and the unmaking of a composite culture. The valley has been assaulted by militancy, the politics of exodus of the Hindu migrants, the actions of the Indian State, the actions of other states. Can it even breathe and exhale its spirit? Yet it is the home of a great intermingling, a philosophical sharing, poetry and suffering. It is still so beautiful that it is often painful. I first went to Kashmir in the late 1980s to chronicle its composite culture; I returned many times since as a journalist to cover militancy, people's protests, the stories of their deaths and suffering in the often cruel circumstances that are now a permanent part of life in the valley. I have seen the most beautiful sights in Kashmir and have also been hauled up and held at the barrel of the gun of the Indian army.

This year, in 2012, tourism is booming and they say that 'normalcy' could have fleetingly returned to Kashmir. But first, who is a Kashmiri and what is Kashmiriyat? The phrase usually refers to an identity that cuts across religious divides and suggests a pluralism in culture and great tolerance. Kashmiriyat also refers to the love of the language and the land. Many works on Kashmiris describe the culture as a composite of Shaivite, Bhakti and Islamic Sufi traditions.

But is Kashmiriyat a historical promise that has not been realized? It is, after all, the land of Lal Ded, the fourteenth-century Shaivite mystic who influenced so much of Kashmiri consciousness. She was a seeker who was a great influence on the Sufi mysticism that would define Islam in the region for years to come. There are lovely translations of her work, a fascinating insight into her search in the context of the history of Kashmir in the wonderful work *I, Lalla* by Ranjit Hoskote:

> *I wore myself out, looking for myself.*
> *No one could have worked harder to break the code.*
> *I lost myself in myself and found a wine cellar. Nectar, I tell you.*
> *There were jars and jars of the good stuff, and no one to drink it.*

Hers is not some inaccessible poetry understood by a few. Ask about composite culture and the first name everyone in Kashmir comes up with is Lal Ded, the Shaivite mystic who is said to have deeply influenced the thinking of Nundreshi or the Sufi Nuruddin, one of the most important Islamic teachers to have spread the faith in the valley. The relationship between Nundreshi and Lal Ded is described as that between mother and son, although there is some historical confusion about the precise dates. Yet there is no confusion over the fact that this is the tradition most Kashmiris say defines their cultural space.

Again, Kashmir is another area where Islam was defined by the Sufi approach and those who embraced the faith also maintained a close relationship with local shrines.

Generations of Sufis belonging to different silsilas brought Islam to the region. The opposition to popular Sufism was launched by the Ahl-i-Hadees and Jamaat-i-Islami but the Sufi approach remained the dominant form of religious expression. That is, however, changing due to recent history. The influence of conservative Islamic movements that spurn Sufi traditions has undoubtedly expanded, as has the power of political forces that promote this more fundamentalist understanding of Islam. The militant movement against Indian authority may also have led to a curious dichotomy in the valley where followers of popular Sufi traditions may have inadvertently supported the political aims of groups who also openly seek to impose a particular code and understanding of Islam.

Along the way, many things have changed in Kashmir. During one of my early trips to the valley in the 1980s, before the separatist movement consumed life in the region, I had climbed all the way to the Amarnath cave. At that time, a four-hundred-year-old tradition linked a Kashmiri Muslim family to this holiest of Hindu holies. The mysterious Amarnath cave, believed to be the abode of Lord Shiva, was discovered by a Muslim shepherd named Adam Malik some four hundred years ago and till some years ago, his descendants were appointed as caretakers of the cave and got one-third of the offerings.

The traditional yatra route begins from Pahalgam and takes three and a half days to reach the cave with night halts at

Chandanwari, Sheshnag and Panchtarni. As mountain paths go, this route is tolerable. There is another route, however, that is far more treacherous. The only reason for taking this path is that one can reach the cave and return in just a day.

This is the route I took. It began from Sonemarg and involved climbing from 9,000 feet to the cave located at a height of 14,000 feet and descending in about twelve hours. Though short, this route is dangerous and every year, a few pilgrims or trekkers slip on the glaciers into the gorge below. Four of us, therefore, took four guides and ponies. Two hours into the journey and the path lay buried in a sheet of snow. The ponies began to slip. The rest of the journey could only be made on foot. Our guides hammered a path through the ice and we crossed the glaciers in a human chain, four novices between four firm-footed mountain men.

Ghulam Rasool, the leader of our little team kept shouting: 'Don't look down. Never look down.' Whenever the path cleared and we did dare to look at the gorge below, the sight was breathtaking—mountain springs gurgling under ice bridges only to vanish suddenly in a sheet of snow. The landscape, too, began to change gradually. Patches of green gave way to the stark beauty of desert mountains where nothing green grows.

The cave itself was an eerie formation wedged between two mountain ranges. Inside the cave, water dripped slowly onto the three stalagmites shaped like ice lingams. The largest symbolises Shiva while the other two represent Parvati and Ganesh. According to legend, Shiva unfolded the secrets of salvation to Parvati in this cave.

The descent was even more gruelling. Our knees began to lock with the sheer strain of climbing. As our stamina gave way and muscles began to jam, the guides had to literally drag us down the mountainside. I fell and began to slip down a glacier. Ghulam Rasool and Sikander Baksh raced down and hauled me up. They kept up our spirits by telling us how lucky we were: there had been no landslide, common in such terrain, and that none of us had problems breathing in the thin mountain air. After negotiating a particularly tricky stretch, a friend turned to me and said: 'Do you realize that our lives are in their hands?'

Muslim porters, guides and pony men have always been a crucial part of the traditional yatra, simply because it would be impossible for many of the old or physically unfit to reach the sacred cave without their assistance. Moreover, for many Muslim porters, a major yatra such as Amarnath represents a rich source of income.

That year, too, troubles had begun to creep in across the ranges and the Harkat ul-Ansar and Hizbul Mujahideen had issued a call, 'banning' the yatra. I asked our guides, 'Will you go to Pahalgam and help the yatris?' 'This is what we do, it is our livelihood and we will continue,' Ghulam Rasool had replied. Later, on flat land, I had met Mirza Malik, the head of the family now settled in Batkot village of Pahalgam. Speaking about his forefather's discovery of the cave, he had said: 'After Adam Malik found the cave, he led a Hindu sadhu there who realized it is a sacred spot. Since then, all our forefathers have played a major role in opening a route to the cave and helping pilgrims reach it. Finally, it was the Hindu king who gave us the right to collect one-third of the offerings. India, after all, is a country where Hindus and Muslims have to coexist and things are no different in our Kashmir.'

Mirza Malik will probably eat his words today. So will Pandit Shyam Lal, who was the purohit of the Amarnath cave when I had met him in the late 1980s and lived in the Pandit dominated Ganeshpur village in the valley. Then he had said: 'In Kashmir, we have always lived together. We Hindus visit the Muslims dargahs just as they have always participated in our festivals. Because of this togetherness, we have no problem with the Malik family taking a large part of the offerings. After all, it was their forefathers who had found the cave.'

The summer I went to Amarnath was the last year of peace in the valley. Then militancy swamped the State, the yatra was entirely taken over by the government and yatris travelled under the protection of the Indian army. Local Muslims were still used as porters but they were all first cleared by the security agencies. Ganeshpur village, where Pandit Shyam Lal lived, witnessed an exodus of Pandits. I never found out what happened to Ghulam Rasool and the Maliks of Batkot.

What I do know is that the narrative about the cave began to change. Advocates of the Hindutva project began to argue that it is ridiculous to suggest that a Muslim shepherd found the holy cave only four hundred years ago when there is evidence to suggest that the Amarnath cave was visited by pilgrims as early as 34 BC. For instance, in an article titled 'Who Discovered Amarnath?' M. M. Munshi argues: 'Muslim rule was established in Kashmir in 1339 and conversions to Islam started by the end of fourteenth century AD during the rule of Sikandar Butshikan. How on earth [could] Muslim shepherds/ Maliks have discovered [the] Amarnathji Shrine which was visited by pilgrims in early historic, if not prehistoric times?'

Could it be possible that the cave was lost for several generations and later rediscovered? Munshi thinks not: 'None of the theorists is committal about the time the yatra and holy cave got lost, [and have] given conflicting dates about [the] rediscovery of the Shrine. Moreover, theorists...have given contradictory names of the Muslim shepherd who rediscovered the shrine as Adam Malik, Buta Malik and Akram Malik.'

The only name I heard throughout my journey was that of Adam Malik. But this legend is not important any more. The story has changed, and the importance of this little tradition is lost in great changes that have overtaken the valley, once at the cross-roads of civilization, once a region that gave us the most incredible philosophical discourse on religion.

It is perhaps best to end this chapter with translations of some sayings of Nundreshi:

> *Why did you not die after reading the Quran?*
> *Why did you not turn to ashes after reading the Quran?*
> *How did you live after reading the Quran?*
> *Did Mansoor not burn after reading the Quran?*
> *Why did you not die after reading the Quran?*

There is another even more powerful contemplation of religion and self:

> *I turned to the No and Yes of La Illaha,*
> *I turned my Self into revelation,*
> *I abandoned the existing for the ecstasy of existence,*
> *That is how I reached the place without place.*

GIVE MONEY, MEET GOD

It would be a mistake to romanticize religious practice and local traditions. All too often, the crass co-exists with what is believed to be holy.

God comes in many shapes and sizes in India, and proximity to God is often determined by the amount of money in one's wallet. For example, visit the Meenakshipuram temple in Madurai. After taking in the gorgeous sculpture and architecture, all Indian visitors queue up to enter the sanctum sanctorum. At any given time of the day, there is a long line of devotees waiting to have a darshan of Meenakshi Amma. But the purchase of a special 'ticket' allows one to jump the queue. Helpful pujaris usher these fortunate few right next to the idol, while the non-paying devotees have to make do with a somewhat distant darshan.

On the day I visited the temple, an intrepid Bengali made a vocal protest against paying to see the goddess, but unable to whip up any support among the local devotees, he left with his family without the darshan. The Bengali should be equally appalled at the hustling at Calcutta's premier temple, the Kali Bari. Though payment is not institutionalized here, the hustling is merciless. Thousands visit this temple, famous for its Kali in black stone with a golden tongue. As I stood riveted before this magnificently fearsome image, a pandit popped up behind the idol and said in Bengali: 'Hundred rupees or move on.' I refused to pay and he refused to give me any prasad. An argument followed. The pandit stuck to his guns: 'If you don't have money for the goddess, the goddess has no time for you.'

The caretakers of the more popular Sufi shrines share the same approach. Take the dargah of Nizamuddin Auliya in Delhi. Usually a visit to this shrine on Jumerat is a pleasure— a host of qawwals sing in praise of the saint, who was one of the most important Sufi philosophers of India. So detached was Nizamuddin from worldly attainments that the most famous quote attributed to him is: 'When the king comes in from one door, I leave from the other.' His self-proclaimed 'khadims' have a more practical view of life and the annual Urs festival presents them with ample opportunity. As the pilgrims pour in, they stand there blocking their path and demanding donations. These supposedly voluntary donations are demanded in an almost menacing tone. The threat is implicit: if you don't give a donation, we'll see how you get past us and our men. Harassed by the crowds and eager to enter the tomb, many pilgrims are intimidated into parting with large sums.

The holiest of Muslim holies in the subcontinent is the dargah of Moinuddin Chishti in Ajmer. Moinuddin Chishti was one of the earliest Sufis to arrive in the subcontinent and founded the Chishti silsila. Nizamuddin Auliya, too, was one of his followers. Like Nizamuddin, Moinuddin Chishti too, led an exemplary life, characterized by simplicity and detachment. Thousands crowd his dargah from all corners of the country and the Indian subcontinent. But as the old saying goes, 'power corrupts and absolute power corrupts absolutely.' So the more popular the shrine, the more energetic the hustling. And at Ajmer Sharif, extracting 'donations' from hapless pilgrims has been honed into a fine art. Refusal to pay up can lead to nasty exchanges, veiled threats or outright intimidation. Refusal to hire a guide, for instance, led to a nasty exchange with one of the self-proclaimed 'khadims' at the dargah. 'We don't want people like you, who don't want to give anything for the saint.' When his threats did not work, the man satisfied himself with following us throughout the dargah with a group of men who looked less like 'khadims' and more like bouncers.

At the popular Sai mandir in Delhi's Lodhi Road, a gang of pickpockets operates quite ruthlessly. The police keeps making announcements on loudspeakers to guard one's possessions. But the pickpockets are so skilled that they can open a shut bag, whisk a wallet out of a back pocket without the victim realizing it. While doing my research for this work, I had my wallet deftly taken out of my purse at this Sai temple. 'Sabka malik ek', as they keep repeating at the temple. When I filed an FIR at the local police thana, they informed me that several purses went missing every single day.

Intimidation at a dargah, theft at a temple, and I can never forget the sheer harassment at Puri. Here's what happens when you disembark from a train at Puri station: You find yourself immediately surrounded by a group of Pandas. 'We

In Good Faith

will take you to the Jagannath temple,' they declare, trying to elbow out each other. They remain unconvinced by declarations that we are not pilgrims and have come to Puri to laze around on the beach. Attempts to shake them off are futile as they follow the traveller's rickshaws on their bicycles. I escaped the Pandas after finding safe sanctuary in a hotel...only to confront them again when I set off for the temple. Again, the ubiquitous Pandas descended, demanding to know my caste and gotra. 'Madam, I think you are Brahmin lady from Bengal. I do puja for all Bengalis... But perhaps you are living abroad for many years.' Or 'I do special puja for only fifty rupees... For foreigners like you, madam, I have special rates...you have lived abroad for many years, yes? Your gotra please... I will tell you if your forefathers are visiting Puri and having blessing of Lord Jagannath.' It is simpler to hire a Panda than to fight off the entire tribe. For, the minute you place your destiny in the hands of one Panda, it is his job to fend off the other. But the demands for money do not end here. As one is soaking in the beauty of this temple, your Panda will keep prodding you to pay for 'special' prasad, or 'special' sindoor to 'bless the ladies'.

Be they Muslim or Hindu, devotees of a Sufi saint or Goddess Kali, the caretakers of the more popular shrines in our country are all worshippers of Mammon. Big religion is after all, big money.

BOLLYWOOD'S MUSLIMS

It may be downright unfair to start listing the Muslims in the Bollywood film industry, many of whom have acquired larger-than-life personas that transcend religious identities. And the larger question this piece addresses is whether Bollywood can be seen as promoting a composite culture, however inadvertently? When I began work on this project in 1992-93, the film industry underwent some convulsions in the atmosphere that then prevailed in Mumbai after the vicious riots. I remember a piece in an RSS publication that said Shahrukh Khan was being promoted by the underworld, which had gone out of its way to thwart the careers of Hindu actors. Around the same time, the Shiv Sena began issuing diktats to members of the industry, expecting them to turn up and seek its blessings. There was a brief time when it appeared that the Shiv Sena would be dictating scripts, themes and casting choices to the film industry. Thankfully, that moment passed.

When Thackeray and the Shiv Sena orchestrated the Mumbai riots from December 1992 to the first few months of 1993, they set in motion a bloody sequence of events culminating in the Mumbai blasts and the subsequent crackdown on the underworld and its connections to filmdom. At that time, two producers known for their gangland links were arrested, but most with big money from dubious sources remained free as they cut their own deals with the new political gangsters. The word was also put out at that time that Thackeray sahib would be gentler on studios and producers who employed more Maharashtrians and less Muslims. At that time, the city was communally charged and many Muslims who worked as extras, spot boys, or stuntmen in the numerous studios of Mumbai were also afraid of losing their jobs. Some did. As a Muslim writer told me: 'As far as the film industry is concerned, Dawood Ibrahim, who had reportedly masterminded the Mumbai blasts was a shadowy, distant presence. The new Don is all too visible and voluble.' And he was gaining respectability.

The drama being enacted between the Shiv Sena-BJP combine and Bollywood producers in those days was a tragic farce. Actor Sunjay Dutt was arrested ostensibly for possessing illegal arms and spent several years in jail. Every member of the industry knew that he was being punished for the sins of his father, actor and Congress MP Sunil Dutt who had helped many Muslim riot victims. The Shiv Sena declared veteran character actor A.K. Hangal persona non grata for attending 'Pakistan Day' celebrations; their first action against him was to demand the editing of his scenes in *Sholay*. It is no coincidence that, in the film, Hangal portrays a patriotic Muslim; he plays an aged blind maulvi whose son is killed by dacoits and whose most memorable dialogue is *'mein khuda se punchunga ki mujhe aur bete quon nahin diye is gaon par shaheed hone ke liye'* (I will ask Allah why he did not give me more sons to sacrifice for this village).

Overnight, an industry with a long tradition of secularism was brought to its knees by the Sena armies. Terrorized at the prospect of their film screenings being disrupted by the sainiks or cadres of the ABVP, the BJP's youth wing, for some years, producers would go scurrying to seek the blessings of the new overlords. The most evocative statement on the state of the industry was made by a poster put up by the management of Naaz cinema, which read: 'Kshatriya is being revived with the kind permission of Shri Balasaheb Thackeray and the BJP'.

Cinema, after all, is business. In the long term, however, even the aberration of the early nineties could not end careers of Muslim actors, writers and composers. There is an interesting parallel between the Muslims of India and African-Americans in the United States—both minority groups have done extraordinarily well in sports, entertainment and the two film industries. In India, the contribution of writers from the minority community has actually created the language of cinema. Sahir Ludhianvi, Majrooh Sultanpuri, Kaifi Azmi, Hasrat Jaipuri and Shakeel Badayuni created the language of Hindi film songs that transcends all regional barriers. Javed Akhtar comes from the same tradition and still continues to write the most popular lyrics for songs, besides his earlier contribution as part of the Salim-Javed duo when they created the persona of the angry young man played by Amitabh Bachchan and changed the narrative of Indian cinema.

In 1990, I spent some time with Majrooh Sultanpuri, then quite broke, his best days behind him, struggling to support his family. He was a typical product of the progressive writers' movement. From a family in Sultanpur, Majrooh was his pen name. In radical circles of the early post-independence days, he is remembered for the powerful social commentary in his poetry and, like Faiz Ahmed Faiz, is considered a doyen of the ghazal form. In cinema, however, he would write the lyrics for some of the most light-hearted numbers, most memorably all those foot-tapping songs for Shammi Kapoor and the catchy songs for Nasir Hussain productions. I remember Majroohsaab telling me: 'This Hindu and Muslim issue never came up in the industry. It was just the control over the zabaan (language) and who can quickly write which song.' In 1949, along with actor Balraj Sahni, he was jailed for his Leftist views. Because Majrooh refused to apologize for some of his writings, then considered subversive, he spent two years behind bars. But he would later thrive in Bollywood, becoming its most prolific song writer.

As he recalled, once when he was broke, Raj Kapoor gave him Rs 1000 to write the song, 'Ek din bik jaye ga, mati ke mol' (one day you will be sold for the price of the earth under which you will be buried). Although Majrooh, who died in 2000, is remembered for peppy, romantic songs in cinema, his serious works are remembered by all those familiar with Urdu literature.

Main akela hi chala tha janibe manzil magar,
log saath aate gaye aur caravan banta gaya.

I set off alone towards the destination,
but people kept joining me, and a caravan was formed.

Not far from where Majrooh was brought up, Rahi Masoom
Raza was born in Gazipur in 1995. He was a formidable
novelist, his most famous work being *Adha Gaon*, a novel
about the feuding families of a village. Set in an Awadh village
called Gangauli at the time of independence and Partition, the
book wonderfully brings to life the cast of characters, Hindu
and Muslim, the elite and the poor, whose lives are so integrated
that they have not yet internalized the message of separate
identities. Years later, when I met him a few times in his
Mumbai home, he was writing the script and dialogue for *The
Mahabharat*, one of the most popular serialized television
programmes ever, broadcast between 1988 and 1991. Because
the climate in the country was changing, there were demands
made that a Muslim must not be retained as the main
writer for a televised version of *The Mahabharat*. But the
B. R. Chopra production house stood strongly by Raza. Still,
he was troubled by the times he lived in. He died on 15 March
1992; had he lived a year longer, he would have seen Mumbai
brutalized by the riots and the subsequent bomb blasts. It was
a city in which he kept an open house and visitors could just
drop in get a meal and even be offered a bed for the night.

Today, Bollywood has survived that age and its members no
longer have to be self-conscious about their origins. The Khans,
the actors, dominate the industry—scriptwriters, songwriters,
composers, dance directors, stunt artistes, light boys, camera

persons, sound recordists, singers, dancers, many of the best and brightest working in Bollywood, continue to be from the Muslim community. The film industry is certainly the arena where this minority group has done spectacularly well.

Bollywood has always been the living embodiment of syncretism at the popular level. With repetitive monotony, film after film has drummed up the Ram-Rahim theme. The large-hearted Pathan, ready to die for a friend or cause, continued to pop up in Hindi films long after the North-West Frontier Province was severed from India and made part of Pakistan. The loyal old Musalman retainer, the childhood Muslim friend, the kind-hearted kothewali, who more often than not spouted third-rate Urdu poetry, were among the other stereotypes regularly dished out by the Bollywood film moghuls.

Crass as the characterization of Muslims may have been, it was never communal. On the contrary, a film like *Amar Akbar Anthony* put across the 'Hindu-Muslim bhai bhai' message far more effectively than all the 'mera Bharat mahaan' slogans diligently telecast on the national network. Amitabh Bachchan playing a Muslim in *Coolie* or *Badshah Khan*, the noble Pathan in *Khudagawah*—the superstar's grand finale as a leading actor—probably did more to lift the spirits of the unemployed inner city Muslim youth than all the fire and brimstone sermons delivered from the Jama Masjid.

More crucially, Hindi cinema transcended regional barriers much more effectively than any Central Government could ever hope to do. Just travel across the land and hear the language change from State to State, but the Hindi film is understood everywhere. The residents of Chennai may switch off the

Hindi news on the national network, but many will still flock to theatres screening the latest Bollywood blockbuster in spite of their own thriving Tamil film industry. From Srinagar to Thiruvananthapuram, one uniform sound heard across the country is Hindi film songs.

And it is in the area of film music where the Muslim contribution cannot be overestimated. The doyen of music composers who drew from the Hindustani classical tradition is Naushad. Today the numero uno of cinema music is A. R. Rahman, a first-generation convert to Islam, who draws from every form of music—folk, Sufi, classical, western jazz and pop—to create his own sound. If one is looking for more obvious examples of the popular composite culture spawned by cinema, one could point to the endless number of bhajans written, scored and sung by Muslims. Take that all-time classic 'Man tarpat hari darshan ko aaj' from the film *Baiju Bawra*. It is written by Shakeel Badayuni, set to music by Naushad and sung by Mohammad Rafi. In fact, Mohammad Rafi has possibly sung more bhajans than any other male playback singer—'Ishwar Allah tere naam' in *Naya Raasta*, 'Mujhe apni sharan me le lo Ram' in *Tulsidas*, 'Brindaban ka Krishna Kanhaiya' in *Miss Mary*, 'O duniya ke rakhwale' in *Baiju Bawra*, 'Badi der bhai Nandlala' in *Khandan* and 'Meri binati suno bhagwan' in *Taj* are just a few of his innumerable bhajan renditions.

Remember Dilip Kumar playing the errant prince in *Kohinoor*? He escapes from the palace and in the guise of a musician, sings 'Madhuban me Radhika nache re, Giridhark muraliya bajere'. This song is one of the best adaptations of a classical raga to popular music. The music has been scored by

Naushad, the playback singer is Rafi, while the real name of the actor who plays the scene is Yusuf Khan. Dilip Kumar, Madhubala, Suraiya, Meena Kumari, Nargis, Waheeda Rehrnan and Mumtaz are some of the legendary stars of Hindi cinema who came from Muslim backgrounds, while Mehboob Khan, K. Abbas and Kamal Amrohi have been among the most skilful creators of the escapist fare churned out by Bollywood over the decades. And how can one forget the two most memorable Muslims to make it big in Bollywood—the king of comedy, Mehmood, and the unforgettable villain who became a legend under the screen name of Ajit? Even if one were to dismiss mainstream cinema as so much trash rammed down the throat of the common man, let us not forget that the two most polished practitioners of the genre dubbed 'art cinema' are Shabana Azmi and Naseeruddin Shah, both Muslims.

Again, I will expand on the parallels between African-Americans in the United States and Indian Muslims. Like the blacks, Muslims are a highly urbanized community, often confined to inner city ghettos where illiteracy and unemployment is high and crime rampant. But just as the African-Americans have found the music and entertainment industry to be one channel that's open to them, Bombay cinema was one avenue where Muslims faced no discrimination. There are small assaults that happened in the 1990s, but members of the community continue to sing, dance, and entertain their way into the hearts and minds of the common Indian. They are the superstars, the superior writers. They are a part of the composite landscape of the most popular medium of entertainment in India.

CONCLUDING IN GOOD FAITH

The world's second largest Muslim population lives in India, constituting 15 per cent of the country's people. But Islam has had a far greater impact on Indian civilization than the enumeration of Muslims in post-Partition India would suggest. Centuries of Muslim rule during the medieval period left an indelible mark on India. Most of the Muslim rulers who made their way to India, most notably the Great Mughals, were settlers in the land, not colonisers like the British who replaced them. They married local women, built great cities and monuments (the Taj Mahal is an abiding symbol of India), and it was in the Muslim courts that the great classical music and dance traditions of northern India were born. This period also saw the birth of a language, Hindi-Urdu, that is created from the intermingling of several words of Persian and Arabic with local dialects.

We have already seen that India became a cradle for the intermingling of civilizations because of the Sufis who arrived in large numbers in the wake of Muslim rule. The Sufis can be described as Islamic mystics who emphasized a direct personal experience of God. The Sufi missionaries either operated through established religious orders or were individual wandering dervishes known in India as fakirs. Though some orders were orthodox, the Sufis attracted large followings in the subcontinent, primarily because they preached a liberal and humane religion, whose egalitarian principles were hugely appealing to a caste-divided society. In the Indian environment, many of the Sufis also came to be worshipped as holy men, and after their death, their tombs, known as dargahs and mazhaars, were credited with miracle powers and draw thousands of Hindus and Muslims every day. The Sufis use of music as a form of communion with God also added to their appeal, and led to the birth of various music forms in the subcontinent.

When two great religions come face to face, it can often be described as an unstoppable force meeting an immovable object. But in India, something entirely different happened. Not only did entire caste groups and communities convert to Islam but Sufi ideas also lead to the birth of the Bhakti movement that would change Hinduism forever and culminate in the birth of a new religion called Sikhism. The Bhakti movement ran parallel to the Sufi movement between the thirteenth and seventeenth centuries and each drew from the other. Bhakti (devotion) can best be described as a reform movement within Hinduism that emphasised the devotion to God as the sole means of salvation. Like the Sufis, music also played a vital role in the expression of the Bhakti faith. Many of the greatest Bhakti saints have recorded their debt to Sufi thinkers of their time, most notably, Guru Nanak, the founder of the Sikh religion. This is why the Guru Granth Sahib, the holy book of the Sikhs, includes several works of a Sufi from the Chishti order called Baba Farid.

This remarkable fusion of the Islamic and the indigenous took place at the height of Mughal power. It was reflected in art, architecture, language, literature, dress and the development of cuisine. But the most extraordinary example of this composite culture was surely the Sufi-Bhakti movement, which stressed personal piety even as it challenged religious orthodoxy, meaningless ritualism and caste and community divisions. In the twentieth century, Mahatma Gandhi would effectively tap this strain in Indian civilization. His favourite devotional song, hummed by every Indian even today, praises both the Hindu gods and Allah, and asks all to be blessed with peace of mind.

With this history, the Indian subcontinent should not logically have become a theatre of constant strife between Hindus and Muslims. But to resort to another cliché, the sacred and the profane have always existed side by side in India. The clue to understanding contemporary India lies not just in understanding its religions, but also its legacy of years of political mobilization on religious lines. This process began during the British Raj, which followed a clear-cut policy of divide and rule. The creation of separate limited electorates for Hindus and Muslims would eventually lead to the demand for Pakistan and communal rioting would become a regular feature of life in the subcontinent. But even post-Partition and independence, India's electoral democracy would also play its part in dividing people along lines of caste and community.

After the cyclical violence of the 1980s and 1990s, right up to the bloodbath in Gujarat in 2002, do we continue to settle political scores on debates in TV studios and remain indifferent to the divisions within? For all the great disappointments with the avowedly secular republic, we have to believe that the glass is still half full and all around India, there is still a thriving composite culture. It is there in our greatest monuments, our classical traditions, in the food we eat, the language we speak, the songs we sing and even in the films we watch.

Let us consider some anecdotal evidence from history. Mirza Ghalib, arguably the greatest Urdu poet the world has seen, wrote a long poem in Persian on Benaras (Varanasi), showering praise on many Hindu places of worship and called it the *Kaa'ba of Hindustan*. Dara Shikoh, Emperor Shahjahan's eldest son who lost the war of succession to Emperor Aurangzeb, translated the Upanishads into Persian and named it *Sirr-e-Akbar* (the great mystery). He also wrote the *Majma-ul-Bahrayn* (co-mingling of two oceans of Hinduism and Islam). In the Deccan, too, the Muslim rulers tried to understand Hinduism. Ibrahim Adilshah, the centre of whose kingdom was Bijapur, now in north Karnataka, was popularly known as Jagatguru. He knew Sanskrit and wrote poetry in Kannada, Persian and Deccani Urdu.

The story of Indian music is the story of a composite culture. Dhrupad and Khayal are the contribution of Muslims to Indian classical music. Amir Khusro created new ragas and the qawwali form, besides formulating language and poetry. Tansen was the great musician of the medieval period. And in the twentieth century, how can one not mention Baba Alauddin of the Maihar gharana who worshipped at a Sharda mandir, taught Ravi Shankar the sitar, besides teaching the sarod to his son Ali Akbar Khan. He epitomized the zenith of a creative composite culture. Bismillah Khan, who took the shehnai to a new level, and made it a solo instrument at concerts, was a devout Muslim but played at the Kashi Vishwanath temple in his beloved Benaras. There is also the example of Shankar-Shambhu, two brothers who became qawwali singers and sang during every Urs at Ajmer Sharif. In Andhra Pradesh, there was Chinna Maulana who played a temple instrument, the nadeswaram, with the greatest artistry and never saw any conflict of religion.

There is so much else to chronicle, which can only be dealt with fleetingly. Imagine a journey beginning in Delhi at the Nizamuddin dargah. There, one can meet one of the khadims and learn how the saint loved the sights and sounds of local festivals, how he adapted his faith to the milieu in which he had settled and began the tradition of celebrating the harvest festival of Basant at his dargah. In Biha, one can hear the folk ballad where Lord Shiva takes on the form of a Muslim fakir. One may also rest a while at Langa Baba's shrine in Giridih district, where Hindus and Muslims worship together. In Gulbarga district of upper Karnataka at the huge shrine of Bandanawaz Gesudaraz in Gulbarga, the biggest dargah in the Deccan, we will discover that the Muslims do not begin the annual Urs celebration without the participation of local Hindu families.

In Gujarat, the shrine of the Urdu poet, Wali Gujarati, in Ahmedabad was razed to the ground during the 2002 riots, his grave dug up and an idol of Hanuman placed there. Considered one of the great poets of the ghazal form, he died in 1707. Centuries later, a mob destroyed his little tomb and overnight, the road was paved over. Things can be lost so swiftly. But in the Kutch region, communities like the Maul-e-Salaam-Garasiyas, or Rajput Muslims, who have blended their Islamic faith with their original Hindu customs still survive. However, many groups such as these that are a little bit Muslim, a little bit Hindu, come under great pressure from both sides, for traditions that bind are also contested, particularly in spaces that are communally charged.

In the two decades that I have taken to make sense of what I discovered, grappled with this unfinished project, tried to make sense of the stories I came across, I've come to believe that, in the midst of the greatest sorrow, there is always a little glimmer of hope.

GLOSSARY

Basti	:	A ghetto or a hovel.
Bhadralok	:	A Bengali term for middle and upper classes of society.
BJP	:	Bharatiya Janata Party.
Chaddar	:	A cloth used to cover the head by Hindu or Muslim women.
Chirag	:	Light.
CPI	:	Communist Party of India.
Fakir	:	A Muslim Sufi ascetic.
Gopuram	:	A monumental, ornate tower found at the entrance of temples, especially in South India.
Hindu Mahasabha	:	Formed in Fiji in 1926, it was an organization that represented all Hindu organizations at the time.
Hindutva	:	A philosophy coined by Vinayak Damodar Sarvarkar that advocates Hindu nationalism.

IPTA	:	Indian People's Theatre Association
Khanqah	:	A building specifically designed for Sufi gatherings.
Mata	:	Mother.
MLA	:	Member of the Legislative Assembly.
Mohalla	:	An area of a town or village.
MP	:	Member of Parliament.
Musalman	:	Urdu word for Muslim.
Mutt	:	A religious institution.
Nikaah	:	A Muslim wedding ceremony.
Prasad	:	Gift from God.
Ram Janmabhoomi	:	Birthplace of Lord Rama.
Sajjada Nashin	:	The descendant of a Sufi Pir who tends to the shrine which is erected over the Pir's grave.
Samaroh	:	A public or social ceremony or gathering.
Sangh Parivar	:	Hindu nationalist organizations affiliated to or inspired by the Rashtriya Swayamsevak Sangh (RSS).
Trishul	:	A trident.
UPA	:	United Progressive Alliance.
Urs	:	Death anniversary of a Sufi saint.
Vaishnavism	:	A branch of Hinduism, it is based on the veneration of Vishnu.

ACKNOWLEDGEMENTS

I will always be indebted to my father, Saeed, for giving me a world of ideas, reciting poetry I often did not understand and for just raising us in his chaotic, colourful, generous world of good food, great talk and more talk. My mother, Aruna, for actually organizing those fantastic meals, for being the most loving Naani to Sara, and for being the pillar around whom we all converge: rested, restless or wounded from our adventures of life. To Prashun, for being the patient companion on this incredible journey, for having believed in my brainstorms, and for just quitting the regular life and taking off with me, thank you again. To my incredible and large family, in which I have found some of my best friends, and to all my friends everywhere who are often like family. Most of all, for the incredible people I met along the way. And Prerna Vohra, thank you for being such an efficient and cheerful editor.